TULIP

The Pursuit of God's Glory
in Salvation

 CROSSWAY

WHEATON, ILLINOIS

TULIP Study Guide

Copyright © 2009 by Desiring God

Published by Crossway
   1300 Crescent Street
   Wheaton, Illinois 60187

This study guide is based on and is a companion to *TULIP: The Pursuit of God's Glory in Salvation* (DVD) by John Piper (Crossway Books, 2009).

Cover design: Amy Bristow

Cover photo: iStock

First printing 2009

Printed in the United States of America

Unless otherwise indicated, Scripture quotations are from the ESV® Bible (*The Holy Bible, English Standard Version*®), copyright © 2001 by Crossway. Used by permission. All rights reserved.

Scripture references marked NIV are from *The Holy Bible: New International Version.*® Copyright © 1973, 1978, 1984 by International Bible Society. Used by permission of Zondervan Publishing House. All rights reserved.

The "NIV" and "New International Version" trademarks are registered in the United States Patent and Trademark Office by International Bible Society. Use of either trademark requires the permission of International Bible Society.

Scripture quotations marked NASB are from The New American Standard Bible.® Copyright © The Lockman Foundation 1960, 1962, 1963, 1968, 1971, 1972, 1973, 1975, 1977, 1995. Used by permission.

Trade paperback ISBN: 978-1-4335-0763-2

PDF ISBN: 978-1-4335-0764-9

Mobipocket ISBN: 978-1-4335-0765-6

Crossway is a publishing ministry of Good News Publishers.

VP		20	19	18	17	16	15	14	13	12	11
14	13	12	11	10	9	8	7	6	5	4	3	2

CONTENTS

INTRODUCTION TO THIS STUDY GUIDE

"DOCTRINE DIVIDES; CHRIST UNITES." Many in the church today would echo this sentiment. To them, controversial doctrines simply promote disunity in the body. Instead of spending our time arguing and debating about theology, we should be evangelizing our neighbors, looking out for the poor, advancing the kingdom, and completing the Great Commission. Doctrine simply gets in the way of these important efforts.

No doubt doctrines have, at times, needlessly divided the church of God. But there is another, deeper, more biblical use of doctrine. Paul exhorts Timothy to "Watch your life and doctrine closely. Persevere in them, because if you do, you will save both yourself and your hearers" (1 Timothy 4:16, NIV). Peter also exhorts his readers to "grow in the grace and knowledge of our Lord and Savior Jesus Christ" (2 Peter 3:18), and what is the "knowledge of Christ" if not another way of describing doctrine? Here is how John Piper describes the usefulness of biblical doctrine: "Our experience is that clear knowledge of God from the Bible is the kindling that sustains the fires of affection for God."

This is our conviction: that biblical doctrine awakens, sustains, and increases our love and joy in God. Piper continues, "Probably the most crucial kind of knowledge is the knowledge of what God is like in salvation. That is what the five points of Calvinism are about. We do not begin as Calvinists and defend a system. We begin as Bible-believing Christians who want to put the Bible above all systems of thought. But over the years—many years of struggle—we have deepened in our conviction that Calvinistic teachings on the five points are Biblical and therefore true."

The aim of this study guide is to explore biblical teaching on the sovereignty of God in salvation. We will move systematically through each of the five points of Calvinism, examining relevant biblical passages and asking key questions. Our primary goal and deepest prayer is that God would be pleased to awaken in his people a deeper knowledge of and love for the great work of the gospel whereby he unconditionally elects depraved rebels to be his people, sends his only Son to secure their salvation, irresistibly and effectually calls them to himself by the Holy Spirit, and keeps them in faith until they acquire possession of their glorious inheritance, all to the praise of the glory of his grace.

This study guide is designed to be used in a sixteen-session, guided group study that focuses on the *TULIP: The Pursuit of God's Glory in Salvation* DVD set. After an introductory lesson, each subsequent lesson examines one thirty-minute session from the *TULIP* DVD set. You, the learner, are encouraged to prepare for the viewing of each DVD session by reading and reflecting upon Scripture, by considering key quotations, and by asking yourself penetrating questions. Your preparatory work for each lesson is marked with the heading "Before You Watch the DVD, Study and Prepare" in Lessons 2–15.

The workload is conveniently divided into five daily (and manageable) assignments. There is also a section suggesting further study (see below). This work is to be completed individually before the group convenes to view the DVD and discuss the material.

> Throughout this study guide, paragraphs printed in a shaded box (like this one) are excerpts from a book written by John Piper, or excerpts taken from the Desiring God Web site. They are included to supplement the study questions and to summarize key or provocative points.

Throughout this study guide, we will reference and examine key excerpts from the Bethlehem Baptist Church (BBC) Elder Affirmation of Faith. This document is the defining doctrinal position for Bethlehem Baptist Church (where John Piper is the Pastor for Preaching and Vision) and Desiring God. This document may be accessed online by performing a search for "Our Beliefs" at the Desiring God Web site and clicking on "Desiring God: An Affirmation of Faith."

The second section in Lessons 2–15, entitled "Further Up and Further In," is designed for the learner who wants to explore the concepts and ideas introduced in the lesson in greater detail. This section is not required, but will deepen your understanding of the material. In this section you will be required to read online sermons or articles from the Desiring God Web site, www.desiringGod.org, and answer relevant questions. These sermons can be found by performing a Title Search at the Desiring God Web site.

The third section in Lessons 2–15, entitled "While You Watch the DVD, Take Notes," is to be completed as the DVD is playing. This section includes fill-in-the-blanks and leaves space for note-taking. You are encouraged to engage with the DVD by filling in the appropriate blanks and writing down other notes that will aid you in the group discussion.

The fourth section in each normal lesson is "After You Watch the DVD, Discuss What You've Learned." Three discussion questions are provided to guide and focus the conversation. You may record, in the spaces provided, notes that will help you contribute to the conversation. Or you may use this space to record things from the discussion that you want to remember.

The fifth and final section is an application section: "After You Discuss, Make Application." You will be challenged to record a "take-away point" and to engage in a certain activity that is a fitting response to the content presented in the lesson.

Group leaders will want to find the Leader's Guide, included at the end of this study guide, immediately.

Life transformation will only occur by the grace of God. Therefore, we highly encourage you to seek the Lord in prayer throughout the learning process. Pray that God would open your eyes to see wonderful things in his Word. Pray that he would grant you the insight and concentration you need in order to get the most from this resource. Pray that God would cause you to not merely understand the truth, but also to rejoice in it. And pray that the discussion in your group would be mutually encouraging and edifying. We've included objectives at the beginning of each lesson. These objectives won't be realized without the gracious work of God through prayer.

NOTES

1. John Piper, "What We Believe About the Five Points of Calvinism," an online article at the Desiring God Web site (www.desiringGod.org).

Throughout this study guide, articles and sermons by John Piper may be found by performing a Title Search at the Desiring God Web site.

2. It is possible to complete this resource in less than sixteen sessions. However, this would require the group to meet for two hours per session and complete two lessons per week. If a group chooses to complete the lessons in this way, then the leader could assign selected questions from the two lessons to be studied rather than have the group participants complete all ten questions per lesson.

3. Although this resource is designed to be used in a group setting, it can also be used by the independent learner. Such learners would have to decide for themselves how to use this resource in the most beneficial way. We would suggest doing everything except the group discussion, if possible.

4. Thirty minutes is only an approximation. Some sessions are longer; others are shorter.

LESSON 1
INTRODUCTION TO *TULIP: THE PURSUIT OF GOD'S GLORY IN SALVATION*
A Companion Study to the TULIP DVD, Session 1

LESSON OBJECTIVES

It is our prayer that after you have finished this lesson . . .

> You will be challenged to reflect upon assumptions that you have about the centrality of theological doctrines.

> Your curiosity would be roused, and questions would begin to come to mind.

> You will be eager to learn more about the sovereignty of God in salvation.

ABOUT YOURSELF

1) What is your name?

2) Tell the group something about yourself that they probably don't already know.

3) Why did you decide to participate in this study of the five points of Calvinism?

WHILE YOU WATCH THE DVD, TAKE NOTES

Precious _____ _____ for the most _____ realities in the world.

What amazing statement does A.W. Tozer make about our belief in God and our problems?

According to Tozer, what generally happens to the church before it goes into eclipse?

What key point does John Piper make from Ephesians 1:4, 2 Timothy 1:9, and Revelation 13:8?

Romans 9 is like a _____ prowling around _____ _____ like me.

AFTER YOU WATCH THE DVD, DISCUSS WHAT YOU'VE LEARNED

1) Which of John Piper's four introductory remarks resonated with you the most? Why?

2) Piper argues that everything exists to praise the glory of God's grace. Interact with the implication of this point, namely, that "sin was planned by God." Do you agree or disagree?

3) Review the essence of Tozer's argument. Do you think that he accurately summarizes the relationship between belief in God and our daily problems? What about the relationship between doctrinal drift and the eclipse of the church?

AFTER YOU DISCUSS, MAKE APPLICATION

1) What was the most meaningful part of this lesson for you? Was there a sentence, concept, or idea that really struck you? Why? Record your thoughts in the space below.

2) As we begin this study, we are in desperate need of God's help. The issues involved are often complex. Therefore, we must pray that God would open our eyes and our hearts to behold and delight in biblical truth and that God would keep us from error. Write your own prayer for yourself and the others in your group, expressing your desire for this study.

LESSON 2
A SUMMARY OF THE FIVE POINTS OF CALVINISM
A Companion Study to the TULIP DVD, Session 2

LESSON OBJECTIVES

It is our prayer that after you have finished this lesson . . .

> › You will reflect on core assumptions to aid you as you seek to study controversial issues.

> › You will understand the need to wrestle through difficult and controversial doctrines.

> › You will grasp the importance of thinking for the life of faith.

BEFORE YOU WATCH THE DVD, STUDY AND PREPARE

DAY 1: INITIAL ASSUMPTIONS AND BIBLICAL AUTHORITY

The central aim of this course is to provide a basic introduction to the five points of Calvinism. But before we can examine the doctrines themselves, we must first establish some introductory assumptions about how we should proceed.

QUESTION 1: In the space below, record your thoughts about what assumptions we should have as we begin this study. How should we as Christians resolve doctrinal controversies? What methods should we employ as we seek to build our doctrinal beliefs?

One of the foundational assumptions for this study guide is the supreme authority of the Bible. Read the following excerpt from the BBC Elder Affirmation of Faith.

> **SCRIPTURE, THE WORD OF GOD WRITTEN**
> 1.2 We believe that God's intentions, revealed in the Bible, are the supreme and final authority in testing all claims about what is true and what is right. In matters not addressed by the Bible, what is true and right is assessed by criteria consistent with the teachings of Scripture.

QUESTION 2: Why is it so important to establish the Scriptures as the supreme and final authority in testing all claims about what is true and right? What alternative authorities might we be tempted to establish as supreme?

DAY 2: SHOULD WE FOCUS ON DIVISIVE DOCTRINES?

It's no secret that the five points of Calvinism have produced their share of controversy throughout church history. Some Christians look upon all doctrinal disagreements as pointless distractions that keep us from the work of ministry. Other Christians stress the need for clear thinking with respect to doctrinal matters for the sake of responding appropriately to God's revelation.

QUESTION 3: Interact with the following statement: "Doctrine divides; Christ unites." Do you agree with this statement? Should Christians avoid doctrinal controversies?

We've already mentioned the necessity of deriving our doctrinal convictions from the Scriptures. However, while the Scriptures are the ultimate authority for Christians, the Scriptures themselves testify to the need for something more if we are to embrace God's truth.

Study 1 Corinthians 2:12–16.

1 CORINTHIANS 2:12–16

[12] *Now we have received not the spirit of the world, but the Spirit who is from God, that we might understand the things freely given us by God.* [13] *And we impart this in words not taught by human wisdom but taught by the Spirit, interpreting spiritual truths to those who are spiritual.* [14] *The natural person does not accept the things of the Spirit of God, for they are folly to him, and he is not able to understand them because*

they are spiritually discerned. [15] The spiritual person judges all things, but is himself to be judged by no one. [16] "For who has understood the mind of the Lord so as to instruct him?" But we have the mind of Christ.

QUESTION 4: According to this passage, what is necessary for us to have if we are to accept the things of God? Underline the key phrases.

DAY 3: THINK! THINK! THINK!

A study like this requires considerable mental effort. Thinking, meditating, reflecting, and questioning will all be necessary as we wrestle through the doctrines of grace. Is such rigorous mental work compatible with the teaching of Jesus in the gospels? "Truly, I say to you, unless you turn and become like children, you will never enter the kingdom of heaven" (Matthew 18:3).

QUESTION 5: How would you respond to someone who dismissed the need to study difficult doctrines because of Jesus' call to become like children? If all that is needed is "faith like a child," then is it right for us to demand serious mental effort?

Meditate on 2 Timothy 2:7.

2 TIMOTHY 2:7

> 7 *Think over what I say, for the Lord will give you understanding in everything.*

QUESTION 6: What is the command in this verse? How does Paul support this command? What is the key "connecting word"?

"Think over what I say, for the Lord will grant you understanding in everything." Yes, it is the Lord who gives understanding. But he does it through our God-given thinking and the efforts we make, with prayer, to think hard about what the Bible says.[1]

DAY 4: THE SECRET THINGS BELONG TO THE LORD

We anticipate that some people may question the propriety of undertaking a study like this. As we have seen, some question the need to study Calvinism out of a desire to avoid divisive controversy. Others speak this way out of a desire to maintain the simplicity of childlike faith. A third group might argue that we should come to our doctrinal convictions using only our Bibles. To make use of the teachings of a pastor like John Piper is simply to put our trust in man.

QUESTION 7: How would you respond to someone who questioned your desire to participate in this study because they accused you of simply receiving your theology from the traditions of a man?

A final reason why someone might question participating in a study on the five points of Calvinism is found in the book of Deuteronomy.

Study Deuteronomy 29:29.

DEUTERONOMY 29:29

> [29] *"The secret things belong to the* LORD *our God, but the things that are revealed belong to us and to our children forever, that we may do all the words of this law."*

QUESTION 8: Interact with the following statement: "The Bible says that 'the secret things belong to the LORD.' Attempting to understand things like predestination and election is simply an arrogant attempt to understand 'secret things.'" Do you agree or disagree?

DAY 5: SUMMARIZING THE OPTIONS

As we've already noted, this study will explore the five points of Calvinism. The alternative to Calvinism is often referred to as Arminianism, after a Dutch theologian named Jacobus Arminius.[2] In the last day of this lesson, we will simply list the two options for the five doctrines in dispute.

QUESTION 9: For each of the five points of Calvinism listed below, write your own preliminary summary of what you believe that particular doctrine teaches.

T: Total Depravity

U: Unconditional Election

L: Limited Atonement

I: Irresistible Grace

P: Perseverance of the Saints

QUESTION 10: In the space below, write out what you believe the Arminian alternative would be for each of the five points of Calvinism.

T: Total Depravity

U: Unconditional Election

L: Limited Atonement

I: Irresistible Grace

P: Perseverance of the Saints

FURTHER UP AND FURTHER IN

Note: The "Further Up and Further In" section is for those who want to study more. It is a section for further reference and going deeper. The phrase "further up and further in" is borrowed from C. S. Lewis.

As noted in the introduction, each lesson in this study guide provides the opportunity for you to do further study. In this section, you will have the opportunity to read two or three sermons or articles by John Piper and answer questions about what you read.

Read the Preface to "What We Believe about the Five Points of Calvinism," an online article at the Desiring God Web site.

QUESTION 11: According to John Piper, what is the result of our gaining knowledge of God? Have you found this sentiment to be true in your own life? Describe an instance where this has been true for you.

QUESTION 12: How do you think John Piper would respond to those who minimize the need to study biblical doctrine? What analogy does he use to illustrate the need to see God clearly?

QUESTION 13: Based on your previous impressions of the five points of Calvinism, what surprised you about the way that John Piper introduced this subject? What did you appreciate most about this introduction?

Read the Historical Information in "What We Believe about the Five Points of Calvinism," an online sermon at the Desiring God Web site.

QUESTION 14: What caused Calvinists to formulate their doctrines in five points? What about this historical overview was new to you?

QUESTION 15: How important is the label "Calvinist" to John Piper? How important is it to you? What are the advantages of using it? What are some disadvantages?

WHILE YOU WATCH THE DVD, TAKE NOTES

_____ theology _____ God and _____ people.
What paradox does John Piper identify in 2 Timothy 2:7?

According to the Calvinistic doctrine of total depravity, people are so depraved and corrupt that . . .

In the Arminian view of election, God doesn't _____ who will _____. He _____ who will _____ and says those are the _____ _____.

What is the main difference between Calvinists and Arminians with respect to irresistible grace?

AFTER YOU WATCH THE DVD, DISCUSS WHAT YOU'VE LEARNED

1) How do Calvinists answer the question: "Who makes the decisive difference in whether you use the grace that you have been given to believe?" How do Arminians answer the question? Who do you think is right?

2) In your current understanding, is the new birth the *cause* or the *result* of saving faith? Why do you say this?

3) Discuss the difference between what Calvinists and Arminians believe about the atonement. What is the major disagreement on this issue? Do you have an initial opinion?

AFTER YOU DISCUSS, MAKE APPLICATION

1) What was the most meaningful part of this lesson for you? Was there a sentence, concept, or idea that really struck you? Why? Record your thoughts in the space below.

2) Having heard a summary of the five points of Calvinism and the Arminian alternatives, reflect upon your current understanding of salvation. In the space below, record which side of the debate you currently agree with for each of the five doctrines.

NOTES

1. John Piper, "Why God Inspired Hard Texts," an online sermon at the Desiring God Web site.
2. For more on the history of the controversy between Calvinism and Arminianism, see the "Further Up and Further In" section of this lesson.

LESSON 3
IRRESISTIBLE GRACE: SIX ARGUMENTS
A Companion Study to the TULIP DVD, Session 3

LESSON OBJECTIVES

It is our prayer that after you have finished this lesson . . .

> You will reflect upon what ultimately distinguishes those who believe from those who do not believe.

> You will grasp six key arguments for the doctrine of irresistible grace.

> You will understand and embrace the doctrine of irresistible grace.

BEFORE YOU WATCH THE DVD, STUDY AND PREPARE

DAY 1: WHY DID YOU BELIEVE?

Though the TULIP acronym begins with total depravity, for the purposes of this study, we will begin with irresistible grace. The reason for this is because, in terms of our salvation, most of us begin here experientially. In order to grasp the central issue in the discussion of irresistible grace, we will begin with a story.

Two identical twin brothers are raised in the same Christian home and attend the same Christian church throughout their lives. They are exposed to the same regular gospel preaching from both their parents and their pastor. At age 16, one of the brothers embraces the gospel. The other rejects it. Later that week, both brothers die in a car accident. Immediately they find themselves standing before God. God asks them both, "Why should I allow you to enter my eternal kingdom?"

QUESTION 1: If you were the believing brother, how would you answer this question? How would you answer if you were the unbelieving brother?

As followers of Christ, we know that the only way that we can come to God is through faith in his Son Jesus Christ. Suppose, as the believing brother, you gave this answer. Then God responds, "You answer well. Faith in my Son is the only way that sinful men are able to come to me. But tell me, why did you believe the gospel and your brother did not? You both heard the same gospel message, and yet only you believed. What accounts for the difference?"

QUESTION 2: If you were the believing brother, how would you answer this second question?

DAY 2: THE DRAWING OF THE FATHER AND FAITH IN THE SON

Put simply, the doctrine of irresistible grace simply means that the grace of God is so powerful that it triumphs over our sinfulness and decisively and effectually draws us to Christ. Numerous passages in Scripture teach this doctrine. We begin with the gospel of John.

Reflect upon John 6:44 and 6:63–65.

JOHN 6:44

> [44] *No one can come to me unless the Father who sent me draws him. And I will raise him up on the last day.*

JOHN 6:63–65

> [63] *"It is the Spirit who gives life; the flesh is of no help at all. The words that I have spoken to you are spirit and life.* [64] *But there are some of you who do not believe." (For Jesus knew from the beginning who those were who did not believe, and who it was who would betray him.)* [65] *And he said, "This is why I told you that no one can come to me unless it is granted him by the Father."*

QUESTION 3: Underline every place in these passages that refers to the drawing of the Father. What indications are there in these passages that this drawing is effectual? According to these passages, is everyone drawn by the Father?

One way to see the power of irresistible grace is to understand the origin of saving faith.

Study Ephesians 2:8–9.

EPHESIANS 2:8–9

> [8] *For by grace you have been saved through faith. And this is not your own doing; it is the gift of God,* [9] *not a result of works, so that no one may boast.*

QUESTION 4: What do you think the words "this" and "it" refer to in this passage? Is it right to say that faith is a gift of God? Explain your answer.

The word translated "this" is the neuter pronoun *touto*, which refers not to "faith" or to "grace" specifically in the previous clause (for they are both feminine nouns in Greek, and would require feminine pronouns), but to the entire idea expressed in the preceding phrase, the idea that you have been saved by grace through faith.[1]

DAY 3: REPENTANCE AND THE SOVEREIGN CALL OF GOD

We saw in the last question that faith is a gift from God. Another passage that speaks this way is Philippians 1:29. But is faith the only response of the human heart that is a gift?

Read 2 Timothy 2:24–26.

2 TIMOTHY 2:24–26

> [24] *And the Lord's servant must not be quarrelsome but kind to everyone, able to teach, patiently enduring evil,* [25] *correcting his opponents with gentleness. God may perhaps grant them repentance leading to a knowledge of the truth,* [26] *and they may come to their senses and escape from the snare of the devil, after being captured by him to do his will.*

QUESTION 5: According to this passage, where does repentance come from? Does this fact make evangelism and instruction irrelevant? Explain your answer.

One of the most common ways that the apostle Paul refers to Christians is as those who are "called" (Romans 1:6–7; Galatians 1:6). But what does it mean to be called by God?

Meditate upon 1 Corinthians 1:22–24.

1 CORINTHIANS 1:22–24

> [22] *For Jews demand signs and Greeks seek wisdom,* [23] *but we preach Christ crucified, a stumbling block to Jews and folly to Gentiles,* [24] *but to those who are called, both Jews and Greeks, Christ the power of God and the wisdom of God.*

QUESTION 6: According to this passage, how do Jews respond to the message of the cross? How do Greeks? What distinguishes those who embrace Christ crucified from those who reject him?

DAY 4: NEW COVENANT SOLUTIONS TO OLD COVENANT PROBLEMS

In the Old Testament, God promised through the prophets that he would establish a new covenant with his people (Jeremiah 31:31–34). But what was the promise of the new covenant and why was it needed? Let's take this second question first.

Study Deuteronomy 29:2–4 and Romans 8:3–4.

DEUTERONOMY 29:2–4

> *2 And Moses summoned all Israel and said to them: "You have seen all that the LORD did before your eyes in the land of Egypt, to Pharaoh and to all his servants and to all his land, 3 the great trials that your eyes saw, the signs, and those great wonders. 4 But to this day the LORD has not given you a heart to understand or eyes to see or ears to hear."*

ROMANS 8:3–4

> *3 For God has done what the law, weakened by the flesh, could not do. By sending his own Son in the likeness of sinful flesh and for sin, he condemned sin in the flesh, 4 in order that the righteous requirement of the law might be fulfilled in us, who walk not according to the flesh but according to the Spirit.*

QUESTION 7: According to these passages, what was the problem with the law and the old covenant? Why would there be a need for a new covenant?

What was wrong? What was the flaw? There are two ways to answer that question: from the human side and from God's side. From the human side the problem was unbelief and hard-heartedness (Hebrews 3:8, 15, 19; 4:7). From God's side the problem was that God withheld the sovereign enablement of his Spirit.

Listen to Deuteronomy 29:4. Moses is speaking as he looks back over forty years of rebellion in the wilderness: "To this day the LORD has not given you a heart to know, nor eyes to see, nor ears to hear." That was the ultimate reason why the old covenant was inadequate. God had lessons he meant to teach in the Old Testament and they involved enduring generations of stubbornness and rebellion and hard-heartedness until the time the new covenant should come.[2]

In light of the shortcomings of the old covenant, it is no surprise that God promises something better for his people.

Study Ezekiel 11:19–20 and Ezekiel 36:26–27.

EZEKIEL 11:19–20

[19] *And I will give them one heart, and a new spirit I will put within them. I will remove the heart of stone from their flesh and give them a heart of flesh,* [20] *that they may walk in my*

statutes and keep my rules and obey them. And they shall be my people, and I will be their God.

EZEKIEL 36:26–27

[26] *And I will give you a new heart, and a new spirit I will put within you. And I will remove the heart of stone from your flesh and give you a heart of flesh.* [27] *And I will put my Spirit within you, and cause you to walk in my statutes and be careful to obey my rules.*

QUESTION 8: According to these passages, what does God promise to do for his people in the new covenant? Why is this good news for hard-hearted rebels?

DAY 5: RESISTIBLE GRACE?

Thus far in this lesson, we have tried to demonstrate that God has power to draw men to himself, to call out his people, and to remove their hearts of stone and replace them with hearts of flesh. We call this the doctrine of irresistible grace.

However, what are we to make of texts which describe people successfully resisting God's gracious invitations?

Study Matthew 23:37; Acts 7:51; and Romans 10:21.

MATTHEW 23:37

[37] *O Jerusalem, Jerusalem, the city that kills the prophets and stones those who are sent to it! How often would I have gathered your children together as a hen gathers her brood under her wings, and you would not!*

ACTS 7:51

> [51] *You stiff-necked people, uncircumcised in heart and ears, you always resist the Holy Spirit. As your fathers did, so do you.*

ROMANS 10:21

> [21] *But of Israel he says, "All day long I have held out my hands to a disobedient and contrary people."*

QUESTION 9: Summarize the teaching of these verses in your own words. In light of these passages, can the grace of God through the Holy Spirit be resisted?

It is obvious that certain biblical texts teach that human beings can and do resist God. Yet we have seen that God also removes rebellious hearts and replaces them with soft hearts of faith and that he effectually draws sinners to himself.

QUESTION 10: How do you resolve the tension between biblical passages that teach that God can be successfully resisted and biblical passages that teach that God grants faith and repentance to whomever he will?

The point of irresistible grace is not that we can't resist. We can and we do. The point is that when God chooses, he overcomes our resistance and restores a submissive spirit. He creates. He says, "Let there be light!" He heals. He leads. He restores. He comforts.[3]

FURTHER UP AND FURTHER IN

Read or listen to "The Called of Christ and the Loved of God, Part 1," an online sermon at the Desiring God Web site.

QUESTION 11: According to John Piper, does God call everyone in the same way? How does he prove his point?

QUESTION 12: What does the call of God accomplish in 1 Corinthians 1:22–24?

Read or listen to "Born Again Through the Living and Abiding Word," an online sermon at the Desiring God Web site.

QUESTION 13: How does John Piper use the example of Lazarus to illustrate our part in the new birth? What is the relationship between God's work in the new birth and our work?

QUESTION 14: What three events give rise to the new birth? How does each relate to our being born again?

QUESTION 15: What two "calls" does John Piper mention? How does he defend these two calls from Scripture?

WHILE YOU WATCH THE DVD, TAKE NOTES

How does John Piper address the biblical passages that describe people resisting the Holy Spirit?

In 1 Corinthians 1:22–24, what makes the decisive difference?

What significant detail does John Piper note in 1 John 5:1?

How do the promises of the new covenant support the doctrine of irresistible grace?

What point does John Piper draw out from Romans 9:18–21?

AFTER YOU WATCH THE DVD, DISCUSS WHAT YOU'VE LEARNED

1) How does John Piper resolve the tension between passages that teach resistance to the Holy Spirit and passages that teach irresistible grace? Do you think his solution is accurate?

2) Which of the six arguments did you find most persuasive? Why?

3) Do you think that the doctrine of irresistible grace makes evangelism irrelevant? What biblical passages have you studied that can help you to answer this question?

AFTER YOU DISCUSS, MAKE APPLICATION

1) What was the most meaningful part of this lesson for you? Was there a sentence, concept, or idea that really struck you? Why? Record your thoughts in the space below.

2) Meditate on the story of Lazarus in John 11. How does the story of Lazarus illustrate the doctrine of irresistible grace? Record your reflections below.

NOTES

1. Wayne Grudem, *Systematic Theology* (Grand Rapids: Zondervan, 2000), page 730 fn14.
2. Excerpt taken from "Jesus: Mediator of a Better Covenant, Part 1," an online sermon at the Desiring God Web site.
3. John Piper, "Grace is Resistible . . . Until It's Not," an online blog post at the Desiring God Web site.

LESSON 4
IRRESISTIBLE GRACE: CONDITIONAL LANGUAGE AND BIBLICAL TRUTH
A Companion Study to the TULIP DVD, Session 4

LESSON OBJECTIVES

It is our prayer that after you have finished this lesson . . .

> You will understand the function of conditional language in Scripture.

> You will identify some misunderstandings of the doctrine of irresistible grace.

> You will grasp the mystery of God's work and our work in coming to faith in Christ.

BEFORE YOU WATCH THE DVD, STUDY AND PREPARE

DAY 1: DOES GOD FORCE US TO BELIEVE AGAINST OUR WILL?

We have seen that, when God saves people, he overcomes their resistance and draws them to himself. Many who hear this truth conclude that Calvinists believe that God forces people to believe against their will.

QUESTION 1: "Calvinists believe that God forces people to believe against their will." Do you believe that this is an accurate summary of the doctrine of irresistible grace? Explain your answer.

Study Acts 16:13–14.

ACTS 16:13–14

> [13] *And on the Sabbath day we went outside the gate to the riverside, where we supposed there was a place of prayer, and we sat down and spoke to the women who had come together.* [14] *One who heard us was a woman named Lydia, from the city of Thyatira, a seller of purple goods, who was a worshiper of God. The Lord opened her heart to pay attention to what was said by Paul.*

QUESTION 2: How does this passage demonstrate the truth of irresistible grace? Does God force Lydia to believe against her will?

But the clearest answer in Acts to the question why a person believes the gospel is that God opens the heart. Lydia is the best example. Why did she believe? Acts 16:14 says, "The Lord opened her heart to pay attention to what was said by Paul." Notice four aspects of this conversion.

1) " . . . **what was said by Paul.**" First, someone must speak the gospel. God does not open the eyes of the heart to see nothing. He opens them to see the glory of Christ in the truth of the gospel (2 Corinthians 4:4–6). Therefore, we must speak the gospel. We don't make the new birth happen when we do. But we fit into God's way of doing it. The point of the new birth is to grant spiritual sight. The point of speaking the gospel is to give something to see. New birth is for the glory of Christ. Therefore, God causes it to happen when Christ is lifted up.

2) **"The Lord . . . "** Second, the speaker of the gospel relies upon the Lord. Prayer is not mentioned here. But that is what we do when we realize that it is the Lord who is the decisive actor, not us. We have a significant role in speaking the gospel, but it is the Lord himself who does the decisive work.

3) " . . . **opened her heart . . .** " Since the key problem in not believing the gospel is the hardness or the closedness of the heart, this is where the Lord does his decisive work. He "opens the heart" of Lydia. This means he takes out the heart of stone, and puts in the heart of flesh (Ezekiel 36:26); he says with sovereign authority, "Let there be light," and shines "in our hearts to give the light of the knowledge of the glory of God in the face of Jesus Christ" (2 Corinthians 4:6). So the darkness flies away and the light of truth reveals the irresistible beauty of Christ in the gospel.

4) " . . . to pay attention to what was said by Paul." The effect of the Lord's opening her heart is a true spiritual hearing of the gospel. "Pay attention to" is a weak translation of the Greek *prosechein*. It is stronger than that in this content. In this verse, it is a hearing with attachment. The work of the Lord does not just help her focus. It brings about faith. She was "granted repentance" (2 Timothy 2:25) and faith (Philippians 1:29).[1]

DAY 2: THE TRIUMPH OF GOD

Look closely at the BBC Elder Affirmation of Faith.

THE SAVING WORK OF THE HOLY SPIRIT

8.3 We believe that, apart from the effectual work of the Spirit, no one would come to faith, because all are dead in trespasses and sins; that they are hostile to God, and morally unable to submit to God or please Him, because the pleasures of sin appear greater than the pleasures of God. Thus, for God's elect, the Spirit triumphs over all resistance, wakens the dead, removes blindness, and manifests Christ in such a compellingly beautiful way through the Gospel that He becomes irresistibly attractive to the regenerate heart.

QUESTION 3: Restate the central point of this section in your own words. How does this affirmation avoid giving the impression that God forces people to believe against their will?

QUESTION 4: From this definition of irresistible grace, how would you illustrate the doctrine to someone else? What examples or analogies would you use?

DAY 3: CONDITIONAL LANGUAGE

One of the key questions that this lesson will seek to answer is the role of conditional language in the Bible. By conditional language, we mean the use of "if . . . then" clauses to communicate the conditions necessary for something to take place ("if you do this, then I will do that"). Though conditional language is often explicit, there are times where conditions may be implied rather than directly stated ("pick up your room and I will let you go to the movies").

QUESTION 5: Give some examples of conditional language that Christians often use. You can either use biblical examples, or you may come up with your own summary statements.

Read Revelation 3:20.

REVELATION 3:20

> [20] *Behold, I stand at the door and knock. If anyone hears my voice and opens the door, I will come in to him and eat with him, and he with me.*

QUESTION 6: Though this passage is probably not referring directly to evangelism (note the context), it is a clear example of conditional language. What questions does the existence of conditional language in the Bible raise for the doctrine of irresistible grace?

DAY 4: MEETING CONDITIONS THROUGH GOD'S PROVISION

As we continue our reflections on conditional language, we will look at one biblical story that sheds some light on this subject. In 2 Chronicles, King Hezekiah has just restored true worship in the temple. He now desires to call together all Israel in order to celebrate the Passover.

Look at 2 Chronicles 30:6–9.

2 CHRONICLES 30:6–9

> [6] So couriers went throughout all Israel and Judah with letters from the king and his princes, as the king had commanded, saying, "O people of Israel, return to the LORD, the God of Abraham, Isaac, and Israel, that he may turn again to the remnant of you who have escaped from the hand of the kings of Assyria. [7] Do not be like your fathers and your brothers, who were faithless to the LORD God of their fathers, so that he made them a desolation, as you see. [8] Do not now be stiff-necked as your fathers were, but yield yourselves to the LORD and come to his sanctuary, which he has consecrated forever, and serve the LORD your God, that his fierce anger may turn away from you.

⁹ *For if you return to the* L ORD *, your brothers and your children will find compassion with their captors and return to this land. For the* L ORD *your God is gracious and merciful and will not turn away his face from you, if you return to him."*

QUESTION 7: Underline every conditional statement in this passage. What is the main condition that Israel must meet in order for God to be gracious to them?

Look again at 2 Chronicles 30, this time adding verses 10–12.

2 CHRONICLES 30:6–12

⁶ *So couriers went throughout all Israel and Judah with letters from the king and his princes, as the king had commanded, saying, "O people of Israel, return to the* L ORD *, the God of Abraham, Isaac, and Israel, that he may turn again to the remnant of you who have escaped from the hand of the kings of Assyria.* ⁷ *Do not be like your fathers and your brothers, who were faithless to the* L ORD *God of their fathers, so that he made them a desolation, as you see.* ⁸ *Do not now be stiff-necked as your fathers were, but yield yourselves to the* L ORD *and come to his sanctuary, which he has consecrated forever, and serve the* L ORD *your God, that his fierce anger may turn away from you.* ⁹ *For if you return to the* L ORD *, your brothers and your children will find compassion with their captors and return to this land. For the* L ORD *your God is gracious and merciful and will not turn away his face from you, if you return to him."* ¹⁰ *So the couriers went from city to city through the country of Ephraim and Manasseh, and as far as Zebulun, but they laughed them to scorn and mocked them.* ¹¹ *However, some men of Asher, of Manasseh, and of Zebulun humbled themselves and came to*

Jerusalem. ^{12} *The hand of God was also on Judah to give them one heart to do what the king and the princes commanded by the word of the* LORD.

QUESTION 8: According to this passage, how do the various tribes respond to the message of the couriers? What distinguishes those who respond positively from those who respond negatively? What implications does this truth have for our understanding of conditional language and irresistible grace?

DAY 5: COMMAND WHAT YOU WILL

In this final section, we will look at two more perspectives on the relationship between God's demands upon us and God's provision for us. One comes directly from Scripture; the other, from church history.

Reflect upon 1 Corinthians 15:10.

1 CORINTHIANS 15:10

^{10} *But by the grace of God I am what I am, and his grace toward me was not in vain. On the contrary, I worked harder than any of them, though it was not I, but the grace of God that is with me.*

QUESTION 9: Underline every reference in this passage to Paul's effort and labor. Circle every reference to God's provision and power. In light of this, who was the one "working" in Paul's ministry?

QUESTION 10: The great African theologian Augustine, after being delivered from a life of sin and corruption, wrote one of the most provocative prayers in church history: "Command what you will and grant what you command." Is this an accurate summary of the biblical passages that you have studied thus far? Why or why not?

FURTHER UP AND FURTHER IN

Read the Irresistible Grace section in "What We Believe about the Five Points of Calvinism," an online article at the Desiring God Web site.

QUESTION 11: How does John Piper respond to this objection: "Yes, the Holy Spirit must draw us to God, but we can use our freedom to resist or accept that drawing"?

QUESTION 12: Why does the doctrine of irresistible grace *not* mean that we are forced to believe against our will? What is the alternative to this distorted viewpoint?

Read or listen to "I'm Sending You to Open Their Eyes," an online sermon at the Desiring God Web site.

QUESTION 13: What comparison is made in 2 Corinthians 4:6? What light does this shed on whether God's grace is irresistible or not?

QUESTION 14: What means does God use to open the eyes of the spiritually blind? Cite Scripture in your answer.

QUESTION 15: Examine the list of "Ten Encouragements to Gospel-Telling." Which ones are the most encouraging to you right now? Which ones do you plan to implement in your own life?

WHILE YOU WATCH THE DVD, TAKE NOTES

What mystery does John Piper see in 1 Corinthians 15:10?

Why do some people believe that conditional language in Scripture is an obstacle to the doctrine of irresistible grace?

Does the fact that God fulfills the condition mean that it was not a real condition?

How does John Piper expand the metaphor in Revelation 3:20?

What effect does the truth in this lesson have on John Piper's preaching?

AFTER YOU WATCH THE DVD, DISCUSS WHAT YOU'VE LEARNED

1) What false inference can we make from conditional language? Why do we make this inference?

2) Reflect again on 2 Chronicles 30. What mystery do we see in this story? Do you agree or disagree with John Piper's explanation?

3) Discuss any remaining questions or objections you have about irresistible grace.

AFTER YOU DISCUSS, MAKE APPLICATION

1) What was the most meaningful part of this lesson for you? Was there a sentence, concept, or idea that really struck you? Why? Record your thoughts in the space below.

2) Spend some time meditating on some commands of God that you are struggling to obey. Make a list of them below. Using Augustine's prayer, pray to God that he would enable you to properly respond to his commands and promises.

NOTES

1. John Piper, "How the Lord of Life Gives Life," an online article at the Desiring God Web site.

LESSON 5
TOTAL DEPRAVITY: SIN IS ABOUT GOD
A Companion Study to the TULIP DVD, Session 5

LESSON OBJECTIVES
It is our prayer that after you have finished this lesson . . .

> You will understand what the essence of sin is according to the Bible.

> You will grasp why the "moral" actions of unbelievers are not ultimately righteous in God's sight.

> You will embrace the biblical teaching on the depth of human sin.

BEFORE YOU WATCH THE DVD, STUDY AND PREPARE

DAY 1: DEFINING DEPRAVITY
In this lesson we turn to discuss the doctrine of total depravity. In some ways, the doctrine of total depravity stands behind irresistible grace. Thus, we hope that the next few lessons will shed even more light on the material that you've already covered.

QUESTION 1: When you hear the phrase "total depravity," what comes into your mind? How would you initially define this phrase? What synonyms or alternative phrases could you use to describe it?

A central focus of this lesson will be on defining sin *from the Bible*. This may mean overturning other, unbiblical understandings of our sinfulness.

QUESTION 2: If you asked a non-Christian to define the essence of sin, what do you think they would say? (If you don't know, ask one this week.) How would your answer differ from theirs?

DAY 2: ALL OF LIFE RELATES TO GOD

Meditate on 1 Corinthians 10:31.

1 CORINTHIANS 10:31

> [31] So, *whether you eat or drink, or whatever you do, do all to the glory of God.*

QUESTION 3: What do you think the phrase "do all to the glory of God" means in this passage? How could you discern whether you were obeying this passage or not?

1 Corinthians 10:31 specifically mentions eating and drinking. Reflect on the last meal you had as you meditate on this verse.

QUESTION 4: What does it mean to eat "to the glory of God" and drink "to the glory of God"? In your last meal, did you eat your food to the glory of God? If so, how? What implications does a command like this have for our definition of sin?

When I asked two weeks ago, "Is the Doctrine of Total Depravity Biblical" my answer was, Yes. And one thing I meant was that all of our actions (apart from saving grace) are morally ruined. In other words, everything an unbeliever does is sinful and thus unacceptable to God.

I said that one of my reasons for believing this comes from 1 Corinthians 10:31. "Whether, then, you eat or drink or whatever you do, do all to the glory of God" (NASB). I asked, "Is it sin to disobey this Biblical commandment?" Yes.

So I draw this somber conclusion: It is sin to eat or drink or do anything NOT for the glory of God. In other words, sin is not just a list of harmful things (killing, stealing, etc.). Sin is leaving God out of account in the ordinary affairs of your life. Sin is anything you do that you don't do for the glory of God.

But what do unbelievers do for the glory of God? Nothing. Therefore everything they do is sinful. That is what I mean by saying that, apart from saving grace, all we do is morally ruined.

Some of you then asked the practical question: Well, how do you "eat and drink" to the glory of God? Say, orange juice for breakfast?

One answer is found in 1 Timothy 4:3–5: "[Some] forbid marriage and advocate abstaining from foods which God has created to be gratefully shared in by those who believe and know the truth. For everything created by God is good, and nothing is to be rejected if it is received with gratitude; for it is sanctified by means of the word of God and prayer" (NASB).

Orange juice was "created to be received with gratitude by those who believe the truth." Therefore, unbelievers cannot use orange juice for the purpose God intended—namely, as an occasion for heartfelt thanksgiving to God from a true heart of faith.[1]

DAY 3: LACKING AND EXCHANGING GLORY

If you ask most Christians to provide one verse that teaches human sinfulness, many will respond with Romans 3:23. But how many Christians stop to reflect upon the meaning of Romans 3:23?

Study Romans 3:23.

ROMANS 3:23

²³ for all have sinned and fall short of the glory of God . . .

QUESTION 5: The word translated "fall short" could also be translated "lack." What do you think it means that all human beings "fall short" or "lack" the glory of God? How would you explain this teaching to someone who was seeking to learn more about the Christian faith?

Romans 3:23 is not the first place where sin is described in relation to the glory of God. Romans 1:18–25 provides a much more detailed and extended reflection on human sin and depravity.

Carefully read Romans 1:18–25.

ROMANS 1:18–25

¹⁸ For the wrath of God is revealed from heaven against all ungodliness and unrighteousness of men, who by their unrighteousness suppress the truth. ¹⁹ For what can be known about God is plain to them, because God has shown it to them. ²⁰ For his invisible attributes, namely, his eternal power and divine nature, have been clearly perceived, ever since the creation of the world, in the things that have been made. So they are without excuse. ²¹ For although they knew God, they did not honor him as God or give thanks to him, but they became futile in their thinking, and their foolish hearts were darkened. ²² Claiming to be wise, they became fools, ²³ and exchanged the glory of

the immortal God for images resembling mortal man and birds and animals and creeping things. [24] *Therefore God gave them up in the lusts of their hearts to impurity, to the dishonoring of their bodies among themselves,* [25] *because they exchanged the truth about God for a lie and worshiped and served the creature rather than the Creator, who is blessed forever! Amen.*

QUESTION 6: According to this passage, what is the essence of human sin? Underline key phrases that describe the sinfulness of human beings. How does this passage help to shed light on what it means for human beings to "lack" the glory of God (Romans 3:23)?

One of the most important truths to hold up in the world is that all human beings, even though created in God's image (Genesis 1:27), are corrupted by the power of sin. We are not morally good by nature. We are morally bad by nature. In Ephesians 2:3, Paul says we are all "by nature children of wrath." The attitudes and thoughts and actions that deserve the wrath of God come from us by nature. In Colossians 3:6, we are called "sons of disobedience." We are so disposed to disobedience against God that it is as though "disobedience" is our father. We are chips off the old block of disobedience. We don't just do sins, we are sinful. We are "under sin," as [Romans 3:9] says. Sin is like a master or a king, and reigns over us and in us. Not that it coerces us to do what we don't want to do, but makes us want to do what we ought not to do. We are not innocent victims of sin. We are co-conspirators with sin against God.[2]

DAY 4: CAN UNBELIEVERS DO
GOOD THINGS?

Thus far in this lesson, we have simply tried to show that at the heart of sin is the exchange of the glory of God for lesser things. The reason that Calvinists talk in terms of total depravity is that we seek to define sin in terms of God, and not man. Yes, sin is harmful to people, but the greatest offense of sin is the offense done to God. Human beings have rejected God, despised God, belittled God, and ignored God. We have refused to honor him and give thanks (Romans 1:21) and we have failed to do everything for his glory (1 Corinthians 10:31). Indeed, apart from grace, everything that we do is sin.

Study Romans 14:23.

ROMANS 14:23

23 But whoever has doubts is condemned if he eats, because the eating is not from faith. For whatever does not proceed from faith is sin.

QUESTION 7: In light of this passage, interact with the following statement: "Everything that unbelievers do is sin." Underline phrases in this verse that help you address this question.

Read and reflect on the following story.

> A small organization in a certain country begins to raise money in order to build hospitals and schools for the poorest of the poor. After raising the money, they put their plan into action and construct three new hospitals and five new schools. Hundreds of people in their region are helped by their acts of generosity and charity.

Upon reading this short story, most of us would conclude that the actions of this organization were virtuous and praiseworthy. Whatever our disagreements, aiding the poorest and weakest among us is certainly a worthy aim.

Now read the following continuation of the story.

> By building these hospitals and schools for the poor, this organization hopes to enlist their help in their campaign to overthrow the rightful government of their country and assassinate the lawfully-elected president and his family. Their charitable actions are designed to win the affections of the people in order to subvert the rightful rulers.

QUESTION 8: What is your reaction to the rest of this story? How does it change the way that you view the building of the hospitals and schools? How might this story help us understand the virtuous actions of unbelievers?

Fix this firmly in your mind, sin is mainly a condition of re-bellion against God, not mainly a condition of doing bad things to other people. This is why it is so sad and so point-less when people argue that they are pretty good people, and so don't need the Gospel. What they mean is that they treat other people decently: they don't steal, kill, lie much, or swear much, and they give to some charities. But that is not the main question. The main question is: Do you love God with all your heart and soul and mind and strength? Do you love his Son, Jesus Christ? God is the most important person in the universe. It is not a mark of virtue to do nice things for people while having no love or reverence or pas-sion for God.

Sin is, first and foremost, a resistance to finding joy in God. And that resistance results in a darkened mind that then suppresses the truth and does not understand God. So the mind that is "under sin" does not seek God and does not know God and does not fear God. And it doesn't matter what we do for people; if we treat the King of the universe with such disdain, we may know that we are profoundly "under sin."[3]

DAY 5: A STUMBLE HERE, A STUMBLE THERE

Most people do not view themselves as totally depraved. They may admit that they are not perfect and that they sometimes do bad things, but they also point to areas of their life where they obey God's commands. How should we think about such partial obedience?

Study James 2:8–11.

JAMES 2:8–11

> [8] *If you really fulfill the royal law according to the Scripture,* *"You shall love your neighbor as yourself," you are doing well.* [9] *But if you show partiality, you are committing sin and are convicted by the law as transgressors.* [10] *For whoever keeps the whole law but fails in one point has become accountable for all of it.* [11] *For he who said, "Do not commit adultery," also said, "Do not murder." If you do not commit adultery but do murder, you have become a transgressor of the law.*

QUESTION 9: In light of this passage, interact with the following statement: "I've only stumbled in small things. I haven't disobeyed God too much."

QUESTION 10: Construct an argument defending the following statement: "Sin is infinitely evil." What objections might someone raise against your argument?

FURTHER UP AND FURTHER IN
Read or listen to "The First Dark Exchange: Idolatry," an online sermon at the Desiring God Web site.

QUESTION 11: What does John Piper mean by the "dark exchange"? What is involved in this exchange? Why is it dark?

QUESTION 12: What accompanies the dark exchange? Give concrete examples of these accompanying factors.

QUESTION 13: In what ways is the dark exchange foolish? How have you seen this foolishness manifested in the world? Be specific.

Read or listen to "Proud People Don't Say Thanks," an online sermon at the Desiring God Web site.

QUESTION 14: What is the message of creation? Give specific examples from your own life where you have seen this message. What response does this message demand from human beings?

QUESTION 15: What analogy does John Piper use to describe the essence and meaning of sin? Come up with your own similar analogy that you could use to explain the teaching of Romans 1:18–23. In light of this analogy, why is sin so evil?

WHILE YOU WATCH THE DVD, TAKE NOTES

According to John Piper, what does "do all to the glory of God" mean?

List two ways that we can define "sin."

What controversial conclusion does John Piper draw from Romans 14:23?

God _____ treats anyone _____ . . . We are _____ treated _____ than we _____.

How did Voddie Baucham respond to the student who believed that God was not doing good to him?

AFTER YOU WATCH THE DVD, DISCUSS WHAT YOU'VE LEARNED

1) Why is it important to define sin in relation to God and not merely in relation to man? What negative effects result when we leave God out of the picture?

2) Do you agree with John Piper that "all that unbelievers do is sin"? Explain your answer.

3) Interact with the following statement: "We're always treated better than we deserve." How would you explain this to a child? To an unbeliever?

AFTER YOU DISCUSS, MAKE APPLICATION

1) What was the most meaningful part of this lesson for you? Was there a sentence, concept, or idea that really struck you? Why? Record your thoughts in the space below.

2) Consider areas of sin in your life that you have mini-mized. How has this lesson changed your perception of your sinfulness? Spend some time asking God to convict you of God-dishonoring thoughts, affections, and behaviors. Be specific in your repentance.

NOTES

1. John Piper, "How to Drink Orange Juice to the Glory of God," an online article at the Desiring God Web site.
2. John Piper, "All Jews and Gentiles Are Under Sin," an online sermon at the Desiring God Web site.
3. John Piper, "All Jews and Gentiles Are Under Sin," an online sermon at the Desiring God Web site.

LESSON 6
TOTAL DEPRAVITY: WHAT DOES "TOTAL" MEAN?
A Companion Study to the TULIP DVD, Session 6

LESSON OBJECTIVES

It is our prayer that after you have finished this lesson . . .

> › You will grasp all the ways that our depravity is "total."
>
> › You will understand the reason why human beings refuse to come to God.
>
> › You will embrace the biblical teaching about the infinite and eternal punishment that our sins demand.

BEFORE YOU WATCH THE DVD, STUDY AND PREPARE

DAY 1: SEEKING FOR GOD

In the last lesson, we sought to define sin in relation to God. We saw that sin is ultimately about how we relate to God. More than simply disobeying commands or harming people, sin is the unbelieving and arrogant rejection of God and exchange of his glory. This dark exchange manifests itself in countless ways in our lives (for a sample of specifics, see Romans 1:28–32). We turn now to examine the extent of our natural sinfulness.

QUESTION 1: Interact with the following statement: "Human beings are seeking for God. Even unbelievers seek for God on their own." Do you agree with this statement? Why or why not?

Study Romans 3:9–18.

ROMANS 3:9–18

> [9] *What then? Are we Jews any better off? No, not at all. For we have already charged that all, both Jews and Greeks, are under sin,* [10] *as it is written: "None is righteous, no, not one;* [11] *no one understands; no one seeks for God.* [12] *All have turned aside; together they have become worthless; no one does good, not even one."* [13] *"Their throat is an open grave; they use their tongues to deceive." "The venom of asps is under their lips."* [14] *"Their mouth is full of curses and bitterness."* [15] *"Their feet are swift to shed blood;* [16] *in their paths are ruin and misery,* [17] *and the way of peace they have not known."* [18] *"There is no fear of God before their eyes."*

QUESTION 2: How does this passage help us to answer the previous question? Underline the relevant phrases. How do we understand this passage in light of biblical injunctions like "Seek the LORD while he may be found" (Isaiah 55:6)?

DAY 2: LOVING DARKNESS, HATING LIGHT

So then, according to Paul, human beings in their natural state do not seek for God. The gospel of John takes this a step further.

Read John 3:19–21.

JOHN 3:19–21

> [19] *And this is the judgment: the light has come into the world, and people loved the darkness rather than the light because their works were evil.* [20] *For everyone who does wicked things hates the light and does not come to the light, lest his works should be exposed.* [21] *But whoever does what is true comes to the light, so that it may be clearly seen that his deeds have been carried out in God.*

QUESTION 3: What is the response of human beings to light? What is the response to darkness? Why, then, do men refuse to come to the light?

Not only do men not seek for God, but they actually despise him and his Son Jesus Christ. Because of their love for the darkness, they refuse to come to the light.

QUESTION 4: In light of Romans 3:9–18 and John 3:19–21, how would you explain the fact that some people actually do come to the light? In other words, if men are as bad as the Bible teaches, then how can anyone be saved?

DAY 3: WHERE EVIL DWELLS

In the last lesson, we examined Romans 14:23. We now turn to a similar passage.

Read Hebrews 11:6.

HEBREWS 11:6

> [6] *And without faith it is impossible to please him, for whoever would draw near to God must believe that he exists and that he rewards those who seek him.*

QUESTION 5: Using only this passage, define "faith." Can those without this faith please God? How does this relate to other truths that you have studied in these lessons?

We have already noted the fact that everything that unbelievers do is sin. Romans 14:23 and Hebrews 11:6 demonstrate this fact. But these are not the only places where this truth is taught.

Read Romans 7:17–18.

ROMANS 7:17–18

> [17] *So now it is no longer I who do it, but sin that dwells within me.* [18] *For I know that nothing good dwells in me, that is, in my flesh. For I have the desire to do what is right, but not the ability to carry it out.*

QUESTION 6: According to this passage, what does Paul mean by the "sin that dwells within me"? How does he qualify this phrase?

DAY 4: THE FLESH AND THE SPIRIT

One of the most frequent contrasts in the letters of Paul is the contrast between the flesh and the Spirit. Romans 8 provides a clear example of this contrast.

Study Romans 8:5–9.

ROMANS 8:5–9

> [5] For those who live according to the flesh set their minds on the things of the flesh, but those who live according to the Spirit set their minds on the things of the Spirit. [6] To set the mind on the flesh is death, but to set the mind on the Spirit is life and peace. [7] For the mind that is set on the flesh is hostile to God, for it does not submit to God's law; indeed, it cannot. [8] Those who are in the flesh cannot please God. [9] You, however, are not in the flesh but in the Spirit, if in fact the Spirit of God dwells in you. Anyone who does not have the Spirit of Christ does not belong to him.

QUESTION 7: In the space below make a chart contrasting things that are associated with the flesh and things that are associated with the Spirit.

QUESTION 8: According to Romans 8:7, why does the flesh not submit to God's law? Underline the reason.

> The mindset of the flesh—the way we are by nature, as mere humans, apart from any supernatural help from the Spirit of God—is hostile to God. It does not and cannot submit to God or please God.[1]

DAY 5: WHAT DOES OUR DEPRAVITY DESERVE?

We would be remiss if we did not take a moment to reflect on the fact that our depravity has merited for us an infinite punishment. Many struggle to understand how a finite creature can merit such a horrendous punishment. To them, such a sentence appears unjust.

QUESTION 9: How would you respond to someone who said, "If we have lived a sinful and rebellious life for 70 years, then we should receive a proportionate punishment. Therefore, we should be punished for 70 years"?

The last question in this lesson will provide the opportunity to reflect upon all that you've learned about total depravity.

QUESTION 10: As you look back over the past two lessons, summarize what you think the word "total" in total depravity means.

FURTHER UP AND FURTHER IN

Read or listen to "Why We Need a Savior: Dead in Sins," an online sermon at the Desiring God Web site.

QUESTION 11: What is the difference between being "in the doghouse" and being dead? Why is this difference important? What false impression may be given if we only emphasize that we are in the doghouse?

QUESTION 12: What does the phrase "dead in sins" mean? Does it mean that we are dead in every sense? How do you know?

Read or listen to "All Jews and Gentiles Are under Sin," an online sermon at the Desiring God Web site.

QUESTION 13: What important truth must Christianity hold up in the world? Why do some Christians not want to hold up this truth? What implications does this have for your participation in this study?

QUESTION 14: What does it mean to be "under sin"? How does Paul defend this claim from the Bible?

Earlier in this lesson, we noted that sin is an infinite evil. Many have stumbled over this truth. But they stumble even more when they learn that our sin has merited an infinite punishment. "How is it possible," they ask, "for a finite creature to do something to deserve infinite punishment?" Jonathan Edwards addressed this question in his day.

> The crime of one being despising and casting contempt on another, is proportionably more or less heinous, as he was under greater or less obligations to obey him. And therefore if there be any being that we are under infinite obligations to love, and honor, and obey, the contrary towards him must be infinitely faulty.
>
> Our obligation to love, honor, and obey any being is in proportion to his loveliness, honorableness, and authority. . . . But God is a being infinitely lovely, because he hath infinite excellency and beauty . . .
>
> So sin against God, being a violation of infinite obligations, must be a crime infinitely heinous, and so deserving infinite punishment. . . . The eternity of the punishment of ungodly men renders it infinite . . . and therefore renders no more than proportionable to the heinousness of what they are guilty of.[2]

QUESTION 15: Restate Edwards' argument in your own words. Do you find this persuasive? What questions do you still have about eternal punishment?

WHILE YOU WATCH THE DVD, TAKE NOTES

What are the first three senses in which our depravity is total?

1.

2.

3.

What is the key point in John 3:19–21?

What are the last two senses in which our depravity is total?

1.

2.

How does John Piper explain the "cannot" and "not able" of Romans 8:7–8?

What two analogies does John Piper use to demonstrate the justice of eternal punishment?

AFTER YOU WATCH THE DVD, DISCUSS WHAT YOU'VE LEARNED

1) Of the five senses of total depravity, which are the most easily understood and embraced? Which are the most difficult?

2) Interact with John Piper's argument regarding moral inability. Restate this argument in your own words. Do you agree with this distinction? Explain your answer.

3) What remaining questions or objections do you have with regard to total depravity?

AFTER YOU DISCUSS, MAKE APPLICATION

1) What was the most meaningful part of this lesson for you? Was there a sentence, concept, or idea that really struck you? Why? Record your thoughts in the space below.

2) We rarely reflect on the depravity and corruption from which we were saved. Spend some time remembering and reflecting upon your former sinful state. Think about the punishment that your sin deserved. Take the time to compose a prayer thanking and praising God for your salvation.

NOTES

1. John Piper, "Why and How We Walk According to the Spirit," an online sermon at the Desiring God Web site.
2. As quoted in *Desiring God* (Sisters, Oregon: Multnomah, 2003), 60.

LESSON 7

UNCONDITIONAL ELECTION: GOD CHOSE INDIVIDUALS

A Companion Study to the TULIP DVD, Session 7

LESSON OBJECTIVES

It is our prayer that after you have finished this lesson . . .

> You will understand what is meant by the phrase "unconditional election."

> You will embrace the truth that God has chosen individuals to be saved.

> You will be stunned by the reason that God has chosen and predestined us to salvation.

BEFORE YOU WATCH THE DVD, STUDY AND PREPARE

DAY 1: INTRODUCING UNCONDITIONAL ELECTION

In this lesson, we will begin to explore the third of the five points of Calvinism: unconditional election. When people think about Calvinism, they often think first about election and predestination.

Before we look at the biblical texts, it will be helpful to attempt to define our terms.

QUESTION 1: Define the doctrine of election in your own words. What do you think is meant by the word "unconditional"?

[Unconditional election] is the teaching that God chose, before the foundation of the world (Ephesians 1:4), who would believe and so be undeservingly saved in spite of their sin, and who would persist in rebellion and so deservingly perish because of their sin. In other words, the wisdom and justice and grace of God's will is always the ultimate explanation of what happens in the world—all of it.[1]

QUESTION 2: What objections to the doctrine of unconditional election have you heard? What are the biggest questions that you have about this doctrine?

DAY 2: THE AFFIRMATION OF FAITH

The BBC Elder Affirmation of Faith contains a summary definition of the doctrine of election.

GOD'S ETERNAL PURPOSE AND ELECTION

3.3 We believe that God's election is an unconditional act of free grace which was given through His Son Christ Jesus before the world began. By this act God chose, before the foundation of the world, those who would be delivered from bondage to sin and brought to repentance and saving faith in His Son Christ Jesus.

QUESTION 3: What are the key words in this statement? How do you think an Arminian would modify this statement in order to reflect his beliefs?

No one disputes that the Bible teaches some kind of doctrine of election. The issue has always been in the understanding and basis of election. Traditionally, Arminians have understood election in one of two ways. We will look at the first now. The second will be addressed in a later lesson. Consider one Arminian theologian's description of his understanding of election.

The point is that the election of the church is a corporate rather than an individual thing. It is not that individuals are in the church because they are elect, it is rather that they are elect because they are in the church which is the body of the elect One.[2]

QUESTION 4: Restate the main difference between Calvinists and Arminians in your own words. Based on what you already know of Scripture, which perspective do you believe is more biblical?

DAY 3: CHOSEN IN CHRIST

One of the key biblical passages that Arminians appeal to in support of their understanding of corporate election is Ephesians 1:3–6.

Study Ephesians 1:3–6.

EPHESIANS 1:3–6

> [3] *Blessed be the God and Father of our Lord Jesus Christ, who has blessed us in Christ with every spiritual blessing in the heavenly places,* [4] *even as he chose us in him before the foundation of the world, that we should be holy and blameless before him. In love* [5] *he predestined us for adoption as sons through Jesus Christ, according to the purpose of his will,* [6] *to the praise of his glorious grace, with which he has blessed us in the Beloved.*

QUESTION 5: Interact with the following argument based on Ephesians 1:4: "God did not choose individuals. Instead he chose Christ to be his Chosen One. Human beings then choose to be in Christ."

QUESTION 6: This passage helps us to see the ultimate reason why God chooses and predestines. What is this ultimate reason? Why is it important to keep this reason in mind as we seek to understand the doctrine of election?

I remember teaching a class on Ephesians 1, in 1976, in what we called "Interim" at Bethel College in those days, and working my way systematically through the first 14 verses of Ephesians and having my world just blown open, again. Because three times—verses 6, 12, and 14—it says that he chose us in him before the foundation of the world and he predestined us to be his sons, *unto the praise of the glory of his grace.*

He chose you. Why? That his glory and grace might be praised and magnified. Your salvation is to glorify God. Your election is to glorify God. Your regeneration was to glorify God. Your justification was for the glory of God. Your sanctification is for the glory of God. And one day your glorification will be an absorbance into the glory of God.[3]

DAY 4: THE FATHER'S GIFT TO HIS SON

Discussions of election and predestination often center on the writings of the apostle Paul. And with good reason. Paul wrote extensively on the doctrine of election. We will examine some of his letters in later lessons. But other biblical authors also address this doctrine. In the gospel of John, Jesus himself discusses the doctrine of election.

Carefully study John 6:35–44.

JOHN 6:35–44

³⁵ Jesus said to them, "I am the bread of life; whoever comes to me shall not hunger, and whoever believes in me shall never thirst. ³⁶ But I said to you that you have seen me and yet do not believe. ³⁷ All that the Father gives me will come to me, and whoever comes to me I will never cast out. ³⁸ For I have come down from heaven, not to do my own will but the will of him who sent me. ³⁹ And this is the will of him who sent me, that I should lose nothing of all that he has given me, but raise it up on the last day. ⁴⁰ For this is the will of my Father, that everyone who looks on the Son and believes in him should have eternal life, and I will raise him up on the last day." ⁴¹ So the Jews grumbled about him, because he said, "I am the bread that came down from heaven." ⁴² They said, "Is not this Jesus, the son of Joseph, whose father and mother we know? How does he now say, 'I have come down from heaven'?" ⁴³ Jesus answered them, "Do not grumble among yourselves. ⁴⁴ No one can come to me unless the Father who sent me draws him. And I will raise him up on the last day."

QUESTION 7: This passage refers to a number of different actions of the Father, the Son, and believers. These actions seem to follow a progression (that is, one action leads to the next). Seek to recreate this progression in the space below. Which action comes first? Which comes second, etc.?

QUESTION 8: The word "election" does not appear in John 6:35–44. Nor do the words "irresistible grace." Yet many would argue that the doctrines themselves do appear. How does Jesus refer to election in this passage? How does he refer to irresistible grace?

DAY 5: MY SHEEP HEAR MY VOICE

In the gospel of John, Jesus often refers to his people as his "sheep."

QUESTION 9: If someone were to ask you, "How can I become one of Jesus' sheep?" what would you say? How does someone become a sheep of Jesus?

Reflect upon John 10:24–27.

JOHN 10:24–27

> ²⁴ *So the Jews gathered around him and said to him, "How long will you keep us in suspense? If you are the Christ, tell us plainly."* ²⁵ *Jesus answered them, "I told you, and you do not believe. The works that I do in my Father's name bear witness about me,* ²⁶ *but you do not believe because you are not part of my flock.* ²⁷ *My sheep hear my voice, and I know them, and they follow me."*

QUESTION 10: According to this passage, which is the proper order?

A) First you believe in Jesus. Then, based on this, you become part of his flock.

B) First you are a part of his flock. Then, based on this, you believe in Jesus.

FURTHER UP AND FURTHER IN

Read or listen to "God Has Chosen Us in Him before the Foundation of the Earth," an online sermon at the Desiring God Web site.

QUESTION 11: What are the two ways that we can pursue assurance of our salvation? What does the pursuit of assurance have to do with the doctrine of election?

QUESTION 12: How does John Piper prove that God chose individuals to be saved? Which argument did you find most persuasive?

Read or listen to "God Predestined Us unto Sonship through Jesus Christ," an online sermon at the Desiring God Web site.

QUESTION 13: What is the difference between election and predestination? In light of this distinction, which one is the controversial doctrine?

QUESTION 14: What is the highest goal of predestination? How does John Piper demonstrate this point in Ephesians 1:3–14?

QUESTION 15: What is the great ground of our predestination?

WHILE YOU WATCH THE DVD, TAKE NOTES

How does Piper summarize what he is about to argue?

How does election help in pastoral situations?

How do some Arminians explain the doctrine of election?

How does Romans 11:4–8 argue against corporate election?

_____ is the most predestinarian book of the Bible.

AFTER YOU WATCH THE DVD, DISCUSS WHAT YOU'VE LEARNED

1) What are the main differences between the Calvinist and Arminian views of election?

2) Interact with the arguments for and against corporate election. Do you believe that John Piper adequately addressed this idea?

3) Reflect again on John 10:24–27. What is so surprising about this passage? How does one become a part of Jesus' flock?

AFTER YOU DISCUSS, MAKE APPLICATION

1) What was the most meaningful part of this lesson for you? Was there a sentence, concept, or idea that really struck you? Why? Record your thoughts in the space below.

2) Many people think of the doctrine of election as a controversial and divisive topic. Reflect on Ephesians 1:3–6 again. In this passage, Paul is not arguing, debating, or refuting anyone. Instead, he is offering praise to

God. For Paul, the doctrine of election wasn't merely theology; the doctrine of election, if understood rightly, should lead to doxology (worship). In light of this truth, write your own doxology about the doctrine of election and pray it to God.

NOTES

1. John Piper, "Pastoral Thoughts on the Doctrine of Election," an on-line sermon at the Desiring God Web site.
2. R. T. Forster and V. P. Marston, *God's Strategy in Human History* (Wipf and Stock, 2001), 136.
3. John Piper, "A Passion for the Supremacy of God, Part 1," an online sermon at the Desiring God Web site.

LESSON 8
TULIP: REVIEWING TOTAL DEPRAVITY AND IRRESISTIBLE GRACE
A Companion Study to the TULIP DVD, Session 8

LESSON OBJECTIVES

It is our prayer that after you have finished this lesson . . .

> ‣ You will pause to reflect upon the greatness of the living God.
> ‣ You will review the two doctrines that we have completed thus far.
> ‣ You will understand the crucial difference between moral and natural inability.

BEFORE YOU WATCH THE DVD, STUDY AND PREPARE

DAY 1: THE SOVEREIGN TENDERNESS OF GOD

As we reach the halfway point of this study, we want to pause and reflect upon why we are engaging in this type of rigorous theological reflection. Theology is not an end in itself; theology must lead us to God. Therefore, before we continue, take a moment to meditate on Isaiah 40:10–31.

ISAIAH 40:10–31

[10] *Behold, the Lord* GOD *comes with might, and his arm rules for him; behold, his reward is with him, and his recompense before him.* [11] *He will tend his flock like a shepherd; he will gather the lambs in his arms; he will carry them in his bosom, and gently lead those that are with young.* [12] *Who has measured the waters in the hollow of his hand and marked off the heavens with a span, enclosed the dust of the earth in a measure and weighed the mountains in scales and the hills in a balance?* [13] *Who has measured the Spirit of the* LORD, *or what man shows him his counsel?* [14] *Whom did he consult, and who made him understand? Who taught him the path of justice, and taught him knowledge, and showed him the way of understanding?* [15] *Behold, the nations are like a drop from a bucket, and are accounted as the dust on the scales; behold, he takes up the coastlands like fine dust.* [16] *Lebanon would not suffice for fuel, nor are its beasts enough for a burnt offering.* [17] *All the nations are as nothing before him, they are accounted by him as less than nothing and emptiness.* [18] *To whom then will you liken God, or what likeness compare with him?* [19] *An idol! A craftsman casts it, and a goldsmith overlays it with gold and casts for it silver chains.* [20] *He who is too impoverished for an offering chooses wood that will not rot; he seeks out a skillful craftsman to set up an idol that will not move.* [21] *Do you not know? Do you not hear? Has it not been told you from the beginning? Have you not understood from the foundations of the earth?* [22] *It is he who sits above the circle of the earth, and its inhabitants are like grasshoppers; who stretches out the heavens like a curtain, and spreads them like a tent to dwell in;* [23] *who brings princes to nothing, and makes the rulers of the earth as emptiness.* [24] *Scarcely are they planted, scarcely sown, scarcely has their stem taken root in the earth, when he blows on them, and they wither, and the tempest carries them off like stubble.* [25] *To whom then will you compare me, that I should be like him? says the Holy One.* [26] *Lift up your eyes on high and see: who created these? He who brings out their host by number, calling them all by name, by the greatness of his might, and because he is strong in power not one is missing.* [27] *Why do you say, O Jacob, and speak, O Israel, "My way is hidden from the* LORD, *and my right*

is disregarded by my God"? [28] Have you not known? Have you not heard? The LORD *is the everlasting God, the Creator of the ends of the earth. He does not faint or grow weary; his understanding is unsearchable. [29] He gives power to the faint, and to him who has no might he increases strength. [30] Even youths shall faint and be weary, and young men shall fall exhausted; [31] but they who wait for the* LORD *shall renew their strength; they shall mount up with wings like eagles; they shall run and not be weary; they shall walk and not faint.*

QUESTION 1: Record all the ways that God is depicted in this passage. What analogies and metaphors are used for God?

QUESTION 2: As you continue to reflect on this passage, what is your reaction to it? What do you notice in it that you've never noticed before? How does this display of God's character and glory encourage your faith and increase your joy?

DAY 2: REVIEWING IRRESISTIBLE GRACE

Before we continue our discussion of election, it will be helpful to remember what we have already studied.

QUESTION 3: Summarize, in your own words, the doctrine of irresistible grace. How would you explain this doctrine to someone who was hearing about it for the first time? What biblical passages would you use? What analogies and illustrations would you use?

QUESTION 4: In the space below, record key parts of the story of your conversion to Christ. Note key events and evidences of God's work in your life.

DAY 3: REVIEWING TOTAL DEPRAVITY

On this day we will reflect on the doctrine of total depravity.

QUESTION 5: Summarize the doctrine of total depravity in your own words. What biblical passages, illustrations, and analogies would you use to communicate this doctrine to a new believer?

QUESTION 6: Does total depravity remove our responsibility to love, honor, and obey God? Can someone say, "Because I am dead in sin and blind to the glory of God, therefore God cannot hold me responsible to live for him or see his beauty"? Explain your answer.

DAY 4: WHAT KIND OF INABILITY?

One of the key aspects of the doctrine of total depravity is that human beings, apart from grace, are *unable* to please God or submit to his law. In our natural state, we *can't* come to God. Many stumble over this truth. "How can God hold us accountable for believing and obeying him if we are unable to believe and obey?"

Jonathan Edwards, the 18th-century pastor and theologian, helpfully distinguishes two kinds of inability.

> We are said to be *naturally* unable to do a thing, when we can't do it if we will, because what is most commonly called nature don't allow it, or because of some impeding defect or obstacle that is extrinsic to the will; either in the faculty of understanding, constitution of body, or external objects. *Moral* inability consists not in any of these things; but either in the want of inclination; or the strength of a contrary inclination; or the want of sufficient motives in view, to induce and excite the act of the will, or the strength of apparent motives to the contrary. Or both these may be resolved into one; and it may be said in one word, that moral inability consists in the opposition or want of inclination.[1]

QUESTION 7: Restate Edwards's main point in your own words. What is the difference between natural inability and moral inability?

QUESTION 8: In the space below, construct an illustration or analogy that would help someone to understand the difference between moral and natural inability.

DAY 5: WHY CAREFUL DISTINCTIONS MATTER

Reflect again on Romans 8:7, Ephesians 2:1–3, and John 6:44.

ROMANS 8:7

> [7] For the mind that is set on the flesh is hostile to God, for it does not submit to God's law; indeed, it cannot.

EPHESIANS 2:1–3

> [1] And you were dead in the trespasses and sins [2] in which you once walked, following the course of this world, following the prince of the power of the air, the spirit that is now at work in the sons of disobedience— [3] among whom we all once lived in the passions of our flesh, carrying out the desires of the body and the mind, and were by nature children of wrath, like the rest of mankind.

JOHN 6:44

> ⁴⁴ *No one can come to me unless the Father who sent me draws him. And I will raise him up on the last day.*

QUESTION 9: In light of these passages, why is the distinction between natural inability and moral inability a helpful one? What does this distinction allow us to preserve?

> This is a great stumbling block for many people—to assert that we are responsible to do what we are morally unable to do. The primary reason for asserting it is not that it springs obviously from our normal use of reason, but that the Bible so plainly teaches it. It may help, however, to consider that the inability we speak of is not owing to a physical handicap, but to moral corruption. Our inability to believe is not the result of a physically damaged brain but of a morally perverted will. Physical inability would remove accountability. Moral inability does not. We cannot come to the light because our corrupt and arrogant nature hates the light. So when someone does come to the light "it is clearly seen that his deeds have been wrought by God" (John 3:21).[2]

Jonathan Edwards isn't the only theologian to notice the depth of our moral inability. Read the words of Charles Spurgeon.

> Permit me to show you wherein this inability of man really does lie. It lies deep in his nature. Through the fall, and

through our own sin, the nature of man has become so de-based, and depraved, and corrupt, that it is impossible for him to come to Christ without the assistance of God the Holy Spirit. Now, in trying to exhibit how the nature of man thus renders him unable to come to Christ, you must allow me just to take this figure. You see a sheep; how willingly it feeds upon the herbage! You never knew a sheep sigh after carrion; it could not live on lion's food. Now bring me a wolf; and you ask me whether a wolf cannot eat grass, whether it cannot be just as docile and as domesticated as the sheep. I answer, no; because its nature is contrary thereunto. You say, "Well, it has ears and legs; can it not hear the shep-herd's voice, and follow him whithersoever he leadeth it?" I answer, certainly; there is no physical cause why it cannot do so, but its nature forbids, and therefore I say it cannot do so. Can it not be tamed? Cannot its ferocity be removed? Probably it may so far be subdued that it may become ap-parently tame; but there will always be a marked distinction between it and the sheep, because there is a distinction in nature. Now, the reason why man cannot come to Christ, is not because he cannot come, so far as his body or his mere power of mind is concerned, but because his nature is so corrupt that he has neither the will nor the power to come to Christ unless drawn by the Spirit . . . [3]

QUESTION 10: How does Charles Spurgeon explain the difference between moral and natural ability? What analogy does he use?

FURTHER UP AND FURTHER IN

Look at another quotation from Charles Spurgeon's sermon, "Human Inability."

> Let us enter a little more deeply into the subject, and try to show you wherein this inability of man consists, in its more minute particulars.
>
> 1. First, it lies in the obstinacy of the human will. "Oh!" saith the Arminian, "men may be saved if they will." We reply, "My dear sir, we all believe that; but it is just the 'if they will' that is the difficulty. We assert that no man will come to Christ unless he be drawn; nay, we do not assert it, but Christ himself declares it—'Ye will not come unto me that ye might have life'; and as long as that 'ye will not come' stands on record in Holy Scripture, we shall not be brought to believe in any doctrine of the freedom of the human will." It is strange how people, when talking about free-will, talk of things which they do not at all understand. "Now," says one, "I believe men can be saved if they will." My dear sir, that is not the question at all. The question is, are men ever found naturally willing to submit to the humbling terms of the gospel of Christ? We declare, upon Scriptural authority, that the human will is so desperately set on mischief, so depraved, and so inclined to everything that is evil, and so disinclined to everything that is good, that without the powerful, supernatural, irresistible influence of the Holy Spirit, no human will ever be constrained towards Christ. You reply, that men sometimes are willing, without the help of the Holy Spirit. I answer—Did you ever meet with any person who was? Scores and hundreds, nay, thousands of Christians have I conversed with, of different opinions, young and old, but it has never been my lot to meet with one who could affirm that he came to Christ of himself, without be-

ing drawn. The universal confession of all true believers is this—"I know that unless Jesus Christ had sought me when a stranger wandering from the fold of God, I would to this very hour have been wandering far from him, at a distance from him, and loving that distance well." With common consent, all believers affirm the truth, that men will not come to Christ till the Father who hath sent Christ doth draw them.

QUESTION 11: How does Spurgeon respond to the Arminian argument that "men may be saved if they will"?

QUESTION 12: Spurgeon says that it is the common confession of all believers that they would not have come to Christ unless the Father had drawn them. Is this your confession as well? Would you differ from Spurgeon's explanation in any way?

Read the Total Depravity section in "What We Believe about the Five Points of Calvinism," an online article at the Desiring God Web site.

QUESTION 13: What shocking statement does John Piper

make about religion? Do you agree with this statement? Can you give any personal examples that demonstrate the truthfulness of it?

QUESTION 14: According to John Piper, do unbelievers do good things? How does he explain the "moral" actions of unbelievers?

QUESTION 15: What additional truth did you learn from reading this explanation that you did not learn in the preparatory study or the DVD session?

WHILE YOU WATCH THE DVD, TAKE NOTES

What is necessary for us if we are to see the sovereignty of God as good news?

God has a _____ _____ of all _____.

We are treated as _____, _____ _____.

How does John Piper explain *moral* inability?

You can _____ _____ so much that you _____ do _____.

AFTER YOU WATCH THE DVD, DISCUSS WHAT YOU'VE LEARNED

1) Thus far, have you received the sovereignty of God as good news? Why or why not?

2) How did this lesson help to clarify irresistible grace and total depravity in your mind? What new insights did you gain from this summary?

3) Discuss the distinction between natural inability and moral inability. Do you find this distinction helpful? What remaining questions do you have about this distinction?

AFTER YOU DISCUSS, MAKE APPLICATION

1) What was the most meaningful part of this lesson for you? Was there a sentence, concept, or idea that really struck you? Why? Record your thoughts in the space below.

2) In this lesson, John Piper tells the story of a woman's conversion in order to illustrate the doctrine of irresistible grace. Reflect on your own conversion. Do you see evidence of irresistible grace in your life? If time permits, share your conversion story with the group.

NOTES

1. Jonathan Edwards, "The Freedom of the Will," in *The Works of Jonathan Edwards, vol. 1* (Carlisle, PA: Banner of Truth Trust, 1995), page 477.
2. John Piper, *Desiring God*, 65 fn13.
3. Charles Spurgeon, "Human Inability," an online sermon at www.spurgeon.org/sermons/0182.htm.

LESSON 9
UNCONDITIONAL ELECTION: DOING MISSIONS WHEN GOD IS SOVEREIGN
A Companion Study to the TULIP DVD, Session 9

LESSON OBJECTIVES

It is our prayer that after you have finished this lesson . . .

> You will grasp why God has chosen to elect individuals unconditionally.

> You will see the relationship between unconditional election and the work of missions and evangelism.

> You will be empowered and encouraged to boldly proclaim the gospel in order to gather in the children of God scattered abroad.

BEFORE YOU WATCH THE DVD, STUDY AND PREPARE

DAY 1: THE ABSOLUTE SOVEREIGNTY OF GOD

This study guide is focused primarily on the sovereignty of God in salvation. The five points of Calvinism summarize key doctrines related to the salvation of sinners. However, the Bible's teaching on the sovereignty of God goes far beyond simply saving sinners. The God of Scripture is sovereign over all of life.

Read the summary of the sovereignty of God from the BBC Elder Affirmation of Faith.

GOD'S ETERNAL PURPOSE AND ELECTION

3.2 We believe that God upholds and governs all things—from galaxies to subatomic particles, from the forces of nature to the movements of nations, and from the public plans of politicians to the secret acts of solitary persons—all in accord with his eternal, all-wise purposes to glorify Himself, yet in such a way that He never sins, nor ever condemns a person unjustly; but that His ordaining and governing all things is compatible with the moral accountability of all persons created in His image.

QUESTION 1: What types of things are included under God's sovereign hand? Be specific. What is your initial reaction to a statement like this? Do you believe that it is biblical?

Study Isaiah 40:26; Matthew 10:29–30; Psalm 135:6–7; Amos 3:6; Proverbs 21:1; Proverbs 16:33; and Proverbs 16:9.

ISAIAH 40:26

^{26} *Lift up your eyes on high and see: who created these? He who brings out their host by number, calling them all by name, by the greatness of his might, and because he is strong in power not one is missing.*

MATTHEW 10:29–30

[29] *Are not two sparrows sold for a penny? And not one of them will fall to the ground apart from your Father.* [30] *But even the hairs of your head are all numbered.*

PSALM 135:6–7

[6] *Whatever the LORD pleases, he does, in heaven and on earth, in the seas and all deeps.* [7] *He it is who makes the clouds rise at the end of the earth, who makes lightnings for the rain and brings forth the wind from his storehouses.*

AMOS 3:6

[6] *Is a trumpet blown in a city, and the people are not afraid? Does disaster come to a city, unless the LORD has done it?*

PROVERBS 21:1

[1] *The king's heart is a stream of water in the hand of the LORD; he turns it wherever he will.*

PROVERBS 16:33

[33] *The lot is cast into the lap, but its every decision is from the LORD.*

PROVERBS 16:9

[9] *The heart of man plans his way, but the LORD establishes his steps.*

QUESTION 2: As you read these passages, make a list of the areas of reality that God controls. Compare this list to recent events in your own life. How does this list affect the way that you view things that happen to you?

This "all things" includes the fall of sparrows (Matthew 10:29), the rolling of dice (Proverbs 16:33), the slaughter of his people (Psalm 44:11), the decisions of kings (Proverbs 21:1), the failing of sight (Exodus 4:11), the sickness of children (2 Samuel 12:15), the loss and gain of money (1 Samuel 2:7), the suffering of saints (1 Peter 4:19), the completion of travel plans (James 4:15), the persecution of Christians (Hebrews 12:4–7), the repentance of souls (2 Timothy 2:25), the gift of faith (Philippians 1:29), the pursuit of holiness (Philippians 3:12–13), the growth of believers (Hebrews 6:3), the giving of life and the taking in death (1 Samuel 2:6), and the crucifixion of his Son (Acts 4:27–28).[1]

DAY 2: WHY DOES GOD CHOOSE IN THE WAY THAT HE DOES?

Asking why God chooses in the way he does may seem odd. After all, the whole point of the doctrine of unconditional election is that God chooses individuals to be saved *without respect to anything in them, good or bad.* But why does God choose in this way? Why elect unconditionally?

Study 1 Corinthian 1:26–31.

1 CORINTHIANS 1:26–31

²⁶ *For consider your calling, brothers: not many of you were wise according to worldly standards, not many were powerful, not many were of noble birth.* ²⁷ *But God chose what is foolish in the world to shame the wise; God chose what is weak in the world to shame the strong;* ²⁸ *God chose what is low and despised in the world, even things that are not, to bring to nothing things that are,* ²⁹ *so that no human being might boast in the presence of God.* ³⁰ *And because of him you are in Christ Jesus, who became to us wisdom from God, righteousness and sanctification and redemption,* ³¹ *so that, as it is written, "Let the one who boasts, boast in the Lord."*

QUESTION 3: Underline every group in this passage that God chose. Why might this list surprise some people?

QUESTION 4: In 1 Corinthians 1:29 and 1:31, Paul gives two reasons why God chooses in the way that he does (one positive reason and one negative reason). What are these two reasons?

DAY 3: THE DOCTRINE OF ELECTION IN THE GOSPEL OF JOHN

We have already noted that the gospel of John is one of the most predestinarian books in the Bible. The sovereignty of God pervades this gospel. But Jesus does not often use the words "choose" or "elect." He refers to election in another way.

Think over John 6:37–40, John 17:1–2, 6–10, and 24–26.

JOHN 6:37–40

> [37] All that the Father gives me will come to me, and whoever comes to me I will never cast out. [38] For I have come down from heaven, not to do my own will but the will of him who sent me. [39] And this is the will of him who sent me, that I should lose nothing of all that he has given me, but raise it up on the last day. [40] For this is the will of my Father, that everyone who looks on the Son and believes in him should have eternal life, and I will raise him up on the last day.

JOHN 17:1–2

> [1] When Jesus had spoken these words, he lifted up his eyes to heaven, and said, "Father, the hour has come; glorify your Son that the Son may glorify you, [2] since you have given him authority over all flesh, to give eternal life to all whom you have given him."

JOHN 17:6–10

> [6] I have manifested your name to the people whom you gave me out of the world. Yours they were, and you gave them to me, and they have kept your word. [7] Now they know that everything that you have given me is from you. [8] For I have given them the words that you gave me, and they have received them and have come to know in truth that I came from you; and they have believed that you sent me. [9] I am praying for them. I am not

*praying for the world but for those whom you have given me, for they are yours. * *All mine are yours, and yours are mine, and I am glorified in them.*

JOHN 17:24–26

*Father, I desire that they also, whom you have given me, may be with me where I am, to see my glory that you have given me because you loved me before the foundation of the world. * *O righteous Father, even though the world does not know you, I know you, and these know that you have sent me. * *I made known to them your name, and I will continue to make it known, that the love with which you have loved me may be in them, and I in them."*

QUESTION 5: Underline every reference to the doctrine of election in these verses. How does Jesus refer to his Father's choice of people to believe in him?

QUESTION 6: Look again at the passages from John's gospel. What does Jesus promise to do for those whom the Father has given him? What is Jesus' desire for them? How can this encourage us in our faith?

DAY 4: ON A MISSION FROM A SOVEREIGN GOD

When some Christians are first told about the doctrine of unconditional election, they fear that it will undermine missions and evangelism. They assume that if God has chosen who will be saved, then our efforts to evangelize the world are superfluous and unnecessary. Therefore, they worry that those who gladly embrace the doctrine of unconditional election will flag in their zeal for world missions.

But is this so? Does a strong belief in the doctrine of unconditional election lead to laziness in evangelism and missions?

Study John 10:14–16.

JOHN 10:14–16

14 I am the good shepherd. I know my own and my own know me, 15 just as the Father knows me and I know the Father; and I lay down my life for the sheep. 16 And I have other sheep that are not of this fold. I must bring them also, and they will listen to my voice. So there will be one flock, one shepherd.

QUESTION 7: How does this passage connect the sovereignty of Christ to world missions? How has Jesus chosen to bring in his "other" sheep?

Start with these words: "I have other sheep that are not of this fold." Christ has people in the world besides those already converted—other people besides us. There will always be people who argue that the doctrine of God's sovereignty over the will of man makes local evangelism and foreign missions unnecessary. If God chooses his sheep before they believe, why evangelize the lost in Minneapolis? But the fact is, the sovereignty of God over the wills of men doesn't make evangelism unnecessary; it makes it hopeful.

John Alexander, a former president of Inter-Varsity said in a message at Urbana '67, "At the beginning of my missionary career I said that if predestination were true I could not be a missionary. Now after 20 years of struggling with the hardness of the human heart, I say I could never be a missionary unless I believed in the doctrine of predestination." It gives hope that Christ most certainly has a people among the nations. "I have other sheep."[2]

In our experience, far from undermining missionary efforts, the doctrine of unconditional election has spurred on our longing to see the nations be gathered to their shepherd. This is because the doctrine of unconditional election clarifies what missions is. Caiaphas, the high priest, unwittingly stumbled on this truth.

Meditate on John 11:49–52.

JOHN 11:49–52

[49] But one of them, Caiaphas, who was high priest that year, said to them, "You know nothing at all. [50] Nor do you understand that it is better for you that one man should die for the people, not that the whole nation should perish." [51] He did not say this of his own accord, but being high priest that year he prophesied that Jesus would die for the nation, [52] and not for the nation

only, but also to gather into one the children of God who are scattered abroad.

QUESTION 8: What truth did Caiaphas unwittingly stumble upon? How does this clarify what the work of missions is?

Jesus described the missionary task remaining like this: "I have other sheep that are not of this fold; I must bring them also and they will heed my voice" (John 10:16). The success of their in-gathering is certain. He said that the reason some don't believe the missionary proclamation of the gospel is that they do not belong to his sheep. But "my sheep hear my voice and I know them and they follow me" (10:26–27; cf. 8:47; 18:37). So the remaining missionary task as Jesus conceived it was "to gather into one the children of God who are scattered abroad" (11:52).[3]

DAY 5: "I HAVE MANY PEOPLE IN THIS CITY"

Jesus and Caiaphas are not the only ones who connect unconditional election to the work of missions. The book of Acts contains a strange encouragement for the apostle Paul.

Consider Acts 18:1–8.

ACTS 18:1–8

[1] *After this Paul left Athens and went to Corinth.* [2] *And he found a Jew named Aquila, a native of Pontus, recently come from Italy with his wife Priscilla, because Claudius had commanded all the Jews to leave Rome. And he went to see them,*

³ *and because he was of the same trade he stayed with them and worked, for they were tentmakers by trade.* ⁴ *And he reasoned in the synagogue every Sabbath, and tried to persuade Jews and Greeks.* ⁵ *When Silas and Timothy arrived from Macedonia, Paul was occupied with the word, testifying to the Jews that the Christ was Jesus.* ⁶ *And when they opposed and reviled him, he shook out his garments and said to them, "Your blood be on your own heads! I am innocent. From now on I will go to the Gentiles."* ⁷ *And he left there and went to the house of a man named Titius Justus, a worshiper of God. His house was next door to the synagogue.* ⁸ *Crispus, the ruler of the synagogue, believed in the Lord, together with his entire household. And many of the Corinthians hearing Paul believed and were baptized.*

QUESTION 9: Underline every reference to Paul's missionary activity in this passage. What response did Paul's gospel proclamation meet with? Put a number 1 by every positive response and a number 2 by every negative response. If you were Paul, how do you think you would respond to this type of reception?

No doubt the opposition that Paul faced wherever he went could at times be discouraging. No one enjoys being held up to mocking and derision. So how does God strengthen Paul's hand for the work he is called to do?

Study Acts 18:9–10.

ACTS 18:9–10

> [9] And the Lord said to Paul one night in a vision, "Do not be afraid, but go on speaking and do not be silent, [10] for I am with you, and no one will attack you to harm you, for I have many in this city who are my people."

QUESTION 10: What encouragement does God give to Paul? Circle every reason that God gives for Paul to be unafraid and continue speaking. Where do you see the doctrine of unconditional election in this verse?

FURTHER UP AND FURTHER IN

Read or listen to "Other Sheep Not of This Fold," an online conference message at the Desiring God Web site.

QUESTION 11: In John Piper's partial recounting of the rise of the modern missionary movement, what energized and gave rise to missionary zeal? How does this foundation relate to what you are studying in these lessons?

QUESTION 12: Of the six observations on John 10:16, which ones had you never noticed before? Are there any other observations about this passage that could be added?

QUESTION 13: How does John 10:16 instill great confidence in our missionary efforts? Of the four reasons that John Piper gives, which one is most encouraging to you in your life right now?

Read or listen to "Prayer: The Work of Missions," an online conference message at the Desiring God Web site.

QUESTION 14: What three things must we know if we are to pray for missions rightly and passionately?

QUESTION 15: Why can we not pray consistently for God to save sinners unless we embrace the sovereignty of God? Do you agree with John Piper's argument on this point? What remaining questions do you have?

WHILE YOU WATCH THE DVD, TAKE NOTES

According to John Piper, what is the purpose of election?

Define the "what" and "why" of election.

What emphatic lesson should we learn from John 10:16?

These teachings are not for _____ _____. They are for _____ _____.

How does God encourage us when we are doing evangelism in hard places?

AFTER YOU WATCH THE DVD, DISCUSS WHAT YOU'VE LEARNED

1) How does the doctrine of unconditional election undercut human pride and boasting?

2) How would you respond to those who are concerned that a belief in unconditional election will undermine evangelism and missions?

3) What practical difference do you think it makes if we view evangelism as *gathering* sheep rather than *making* sheep?

AFTER YOU DISCUSS, MAKE APPLICATION

1) What was the most meaningful part of this lesson for you? Was there a sentence, concept, or idea that really struck you? Why? Record your thoughts in the space below.

2) Choose a missionary that you know who is working to evangelize the lost (if you don't know a missionary, ask someone at your church for a list). Pray for this missionary today. Pray that God would be pleased to use them to gather in his people who are scattered abroad, that Jesus' sheep who have not yet been brought in would hear his voice in the missionary's preaching and be irresistibly drawn to Christ.

NOTES

1. John Piper, "Why I Do Not Say 'God Did Not Cause This Calamity, But He Can Use It For Good,'" an online sermon at the Desiring God Web site.
2. John Piper, "I Have Other Sheep," an online sermon at the Desiring God Web site.
3. John Piper, "A Pastor's Role in World Missions," an online conference message at the Desiring God Web site.

LESSON 10
UNCONDITIONAL ELECTION: WHAT ABOUT FOREKNOWLEDGE AND FAITH?
A Companion Study to the TULIP DVD, Session 10

LESSON OBJECTIVES

It is our prayer that after you have finished this lesson . . .

> You will understand one of the key biblical meanings of God's foreknowledge.

> You will have a deep understanding of how the doctrine of election grounds our faith in some of God's most precious promises.

> You will properly grasp the relationship between God's election and our faith.

BEFORE YOU WATCH THE DVD, STUDY AND PREPARE

DAY 1: ALTERNATIVES TO UNCONDITIONAL ELECTION

Not all Christians embrace the God-exalting and man-humbling doctrine of unconditional election. While acknowledging that election is mentioned in the Bible, they have other ways of explaining the basis upon which God chooses his people.

QUESTION 1: What are some alternatives to unconditional election that you have heard of? What is your assessment of these alternatives?

QUESTION 2: Interact with the following statement: "God chooses us because he foreknows that we will believe in Jesus. God's foreknowledge is the basis of election."

DAY 2: WHAT IS FOREKNOWN IN ROMANS 8:29?

Those who believe that God bases his election on his foreknowledge of who will believe often appeal to Romans 8:28–30. They argue that God's foreknowledge of our faith precedes and gives rise to his predestination of us to conformity to Christ.

Examine Romans 8:28–30.

ROMANS 8:28-30

> [28] And we know that for those who love God all things work together for good, for those who are called according to his purpose. [29] For those whom he foreknew he also predestined to be conformed to the image of his Son, in order that he

might be the firstborn among many brothers. 30 And those whom he predestined he also called, and those whom he called he also justified, and those whom he justified he also glorified.

QUESTION 3: Make some observations about foreknowledge in this passage. What is foreknown? What is the result of foreknowledge in this verse?

QUESTION 4: Look again at Romans 8:28–30. What is the connection between verse 28 and verses 29–30? What does this say about the importance of election and predestination for the Christian life?

"For" indicates that verses 29–30 are the foundation for verse 28. They give reasons why we can KNOW all things will work together for those who are called according to God's purpose.[1]

DAY 3: A BIBLICAL EXAMINATION OF KNOWLEDGE AND FOREKNOWLEDGE

In the previous section, you saw that in Romans 8:29, *people* are foreknown. This has implications for our understanding of foreknowledge. The Bible often speaks of "knowing," "knowledge," and "foreknowledge" in very specific ways.

Study Genesis 4:1; Jeremiah 1:4–5; and Amos 3:1–2.

GENESIS 4:1

¹ Now Adam knew Eve his wife, and she conceived and bore Cain, saying, "I have gotten a man with the help of the LORD."

JEREMIAH 1:4–5

⁴ Now the word of the LORD came to me, saying, ⁵ "Before I formed you in the womb I knew you, and before you were born I consecrated you; I appointed you a prophet to the nations."

AMOS 3:1–2

¹ Hear this word that the LORD has spoken against you, O people of Israel, against the whole family that I brought up out of the land of Egypt: ² "You only have I known of all the families of the earth; therefore I will punish you for all your iniquities."

QUESTION 5: What is the meaning of the word "know" in these passages? Provide some synonyms in the space below. Does it refer to "awareness" of something? Or does it refer to something else?

The Old Testament background given above can help to shed light on the meaning of "foreknow" in Romans 8:29. However, there is an even clearer passage that sheds light on the meaning of this word.

Study Romans 11:1–2.

ROMANS 11:1–2

> [1] *I ask, then, has God rejected his people? By no means! For I myself am an Israelite, a descendant of Abraham, a member of the tribe of Benjamin.* [2] *God has not rejected his people whom he foreknew. Do you not know what the Scripture says of Elijah, how he appeals to God against Israel?*

QUESTION 6: What is the meaning of "foreknew" in this passage? What are some synonyms for this word here? How does this shed light on Romans 8:29?

DAY 4: A CLOSER LOOK AT ROMANS 8:29–30

We are not ready to leave off our study of Romans 8:28–30 yet. A closer look at the progression in these verses will help us understand the relationship between foreknowledge and election.

Look again at Romans 8:28–30.

ROMANS 8:28–30

> ²⁸ *And we know that for those who love God all things work together for good, for those who are called according to his purpose.* ²⁹ *For those whom he foreknew he also predestined to be conformed to the image of his Son, in order that he might be the firstborn among many brothers.* ³⁰ *And those whom he predestined he also called, and those whom he called he also justified, and those whom he justified he also glorified.*

QUESTION 7: In verse 30, the word "called" is mentioned. Does this refer to the general or specific call of the gospel (for more on this distinction, see Lesson 3)? How do you know?

QUESTION 8: How does identifying the "call" of verse 30 help to illuminate the meaning of "foreknew" in verse 29? After all of your study, what do you think the word "foreknew" means in this passage?

DAY 5: THE RELATIONSHIP BETWEEN ELECTION AND FAITH

Thus far in this lesson we have sought to examine the meaning of foreknowledge in Romans 8:29–30. We saw that God does not foreknow *faith* in Romans 8:29; he foreknows *people* ("those *whom* he foreknew"). So what then is the relationship between election and faith?

Carefully examine Acts 13:46–48.

ACTS 13:46–48

> [46] *And Paul and Barnabas spoke out boldly, saying, "It was necessary that the word of God be spoken first to you. Since you thrust it aside and judge yourselves unworthy of eternal life, behold, we are turning to the Gentiles.* [47] *For so the Lord has commanded us, saying, 'I have made you a light for the Gentiles, that you may bring salvation to the ends of the earth.'"* [48] *And when the Gentiles heard this, they began rejoicing and glorifying the word of the Lord, and as many as were appointed to eternal life believed.*

QUESTION 9: Where do you see the doctrine of election in this passage? According to this passage, what is the relationship between being appointed to eternal life and believing? Which is the foundation of the other?

Now study 1 Thessalonians 1:4–5.

1 THESSALONIANS 1:4–5

> [4] *For we know, brothers loved by God, that he has chosen you,* [5] *because our gospel came to you not only in word, but also in power and in the Holy Spirit and with full conviction. You know what kind of men we proved to be among you for your sake.*

QUESTION 10: How does Paul know that the Thessalonians have been chosen by God? What is the evidence of their election? What does this tell us about the connection between election and faith?

FURTHER UP AND FURTHER IN

Read or listen to "Those Whom He Foreknow He Predestined," an online sermon from the Desiring God Web site.

QUESTION 11: Why does Paul provide such a deep and theological foundation for his promise in Romans 8:28? Do you see the need for this foundation in your own life?

QUESTION 12: What are the two possible ways to understand the word "foreknew" in Romans 8:29? Which one does John Piper argue for? Which one do you embrace?

QUESTION 13: Which argument for the second view of "foreknew" did you find most persuasive? Which argument was least persuasive? Can you think of any additional arguments for the second view of "foreknow"? What about the first view of "foreknow"?

Read the Unconditional Election section of "What We Believe about the Five Points of Calvinism," an online article at the Desiring God Web site.

QUESTION 14: Does the fact that election is unconditional mean that *final salvation* is unconditional? Why or why not?

QUESTION 15: How does John Piper prove that election is, in fact, unconditional? What would be the alternative to unconditional election?

WHILE YOU WATCH THE DVD, TAKE NOTES

What is the "big question" between the two systems?

What is the Arminian understanding of Romans 8:29–30?

What are two possible meanings of the word "know"?

What is the difference between predestination and election?

What is the key point in Acts 13:48?

AFTER YOU WATCH THE DVD, DISCUSS WHAT YOU'VE LEARNED

1) List all the key synonyms for "election" that you have studied thus far. Provide one Bible verse for each synonym.

2) Discuss John Piper's interpretation of Romans 8:28–30. Do you agree or disagree with his interpretation? Explain your answer.

3) What is the relationship between unconditional election and saving faith? Why is it important to understand this relationship correctly?

AFTER YOU DISCUSS, MAKE APPLICATION

1) What was the most meaningful part of this lesson for you? Was there a sentence, concept, or idea that really struck you? Why? Record your thoughts in the space below.

2) We noted in this lesson that Romans 8:29–30, with its discussion of election and predestination, grounds the great promise of Romans 8:28. This promise is a great encouragement to us when we are enduring difficult times. Reflect on any current suffering or hardship in your life. Now reflect on Romans 8:28–30. What encouragement do you gain from this passage? Record your reflections below.

NOTES

1. John Piper, "Those Whom He Foreknew He Predestined," an online sermon at the Desiring God Web site.

LESSON 11
UNCONDITIONAL ELECTION: ROMANS 9 AND THE TWO WILLS OF GOD
A Companion Study to the TULIP DVD, Session 11

LESSON OBJECTIVES

It is our prayer that after you have finished this lesson . . .

> You will joyfully embrace the argument of Romans 9 as it relates to unconditional election.

> You will understand why it is not unjust for God to choose unconditionally who will be saved.

> You will grasp how we can reconcile unconditional election with God's desire for all men to be saved.

BEFORE YOU WATCH THE DVD, STUDY AND PREPARE

DAY 1: OBJECTIONS TO UNCONDITIONAL ELECTION

Even after people have been exposed to the biblical teaching on unconditional election, difficulties remain. Many struggle to embrace this biblical doctrine. The reasons for this struggle are diverse.

QUESTION 1: What are some objections to unconditional election that you have heard? What questions do you think someone might raise after hearing that God chooses people to be saved without reference to their actions?

Thankfully, the Bible is not unaware of objections to the truth of unconditional election. In fact, there are certain passages in which the biblical authors respond to some objections to this doctrine. Romans 9:1–23 is one such passage. We begin by setting up the problem that Paul will address.

Carefully read Romans 9:1–5.

ROMANS 9:1–5

> [1] *I am speaking the truth in Christ—I am not lying; my conscience bears me witness in the Holy Spirit—* [2] *that I have great sorrow and unceasing anguish in my heart.* [3] *For I could wish that I myself were accursed and cut off from Christ for the sake of my brothers, my kinsmen according to the flesh.* [4] *They are Israelites, and to them belong the adoption, the glory, the covenants, the giving of the law, the worship, and the promises.* [5] *To them belong the patriarchs, and from their race, according to the flesh, is the Christ who is God over all, blessed forever. Amen.*

QUESTION 2: What problem is causing Paul such great sorrow in these verses? What theological problems might this reality raise for Christians?

DAY 2: THE WORD OF GOD HAS NOT FAILED

In the previous section we saw that Paul is grieved at the failure of his fellow Jews to embrace their Messiah. Despite their incredible privileges and blessings, the vast majority of Jews were rejecting Jesus Christ. This rejection by the Jews raised a massive theological problem for Paul: How can we be confident of God's faithfulness to his word if his own people were not being saved? Hasn't God's promise to Israel failed?

Study Romans 9:6–13.

ROMANS 9:6–13

> [6] *But it is not as though the word of God has failed. For not all who are descended from Israel belong to Israel,* [7] *and not all are children of Abraham because they are his offspring, but "Through Isaac shall your offspring be named."* [8] *This means that it is not the children of the flesh who are the children of God, but the children of the promise are counted as offspring.* [9] *For this is what the promise said: "About this time next year I will return, and Sarah shall have a son."* [10] *And not only so, but also when Rebekah had conceived children by one man, our forefather Isaac,* [11] *though they were not yet born and had done nothing either good or bad—in order that God's purpose of election might continue, not because of works but because of him who calls—* [12] *she was told, "The older will serve the younger."* [13] *As it is written, "Jacob I loved, but Esau I hated."*

QUESTION 3: How does Paul demonstrate that God's Word has not failed? Which key events and people in Israel's history does he draw attention to?

QUESTION 4: In verses 11–13, Paul refers to the election of Jacob over Esau. Why is the timing of God's choice important? Why did God choose Jacob in this way?

DAY 3: DEFENDING THE RIGHTEOUSNESS OF GOD

Having established God's choice of Isaac over Ishmael and Jacob over Esau, all in accord with God's electing purpose, Paul then moves to respond to objections to his theology.

Meditate on Romans 9:14–18.

ROMANS 9:14–18

> [14] *What shall we say then? Is there injustice on God's part? By no means!* [15] *For he says to Moses, "I will have mercy on whom I have mercy, and I will have compassion on whom I have compassion."* [16] *So then it depends not on human will or exertion, but on God, who has mercy.* [17] *For the Scripture says to Pharaoh, "For this very purpose I have raised you up, that I might show my power in you, and that my name might be proclaimed in all the earth."* [18] *So then he has mercy on whomever he wills, and he hardens whomever he wills.*

QUESTION 5: What objection does Paul raise and then respond to? Why is this fact important for our modern discussions of the doctrine of unconditional election?

QUESTION 6: How does Paul defend God's justice in verses 15–18? Explain Paul's argument in your own words. Why is it *not* unjust for God to choose individuals before they were born or had done anything good or bad?

DAY 4: A CLOSER LOOK AT PAUL'S RESPONSE

In the last section we looked at Paul's response to an objection against his doctrine of unconditional election, a doctrine that he had unpacked in Romans 9:6–13. The objection was that Paul's doctrine of election makes God unjust. Paul denies this objection and then defends the righteousness of God from the Old Testament. However, Paul's logic has often puzzled Christians. In order to understand Paul's response, let us look at one of the Old Testament passages that Paul quotes.

Study Exodus 33:18–19.

EXODUS 33:18–19

> [18] *Moses said, "Please show me your glory."* [19] *And he said, "I will make all my goodness pass before you and will proclaim before you my name 'The* LORD.' *And I will be gracious to whom I will be gracious, and will show mercy on whom I will show mercy."*

QUESTION 7: Underline key words in this passage. How does God respond to Moses' request to see his glory? What is the main point of the last sentence?

QUESTION 8: How does understanding Exodus 33:18–19 help us grasp Paul's response in Romans 9:14–18? Why is God not unjust to choose individuals in the way that he does?

DAY 5: GOD'S DESIRE FOR ALL TO BE SAVED

Having sought to demonstrate the biblical basis for the doctrine of unconditional election, we turn now to examine some biblical passages that seem to undermine this doctrine.

Study 1 Timothy 2:1–4 and 2 Peter 3:9.

1 TIMOTHY 2:1-4

¹ First of all, then, I urge that supplications, prayers, intercessions, and thanksgivings be made for all people, ² for kings and all who are in high positions, that we may lead a peaceful and quiet life, godly and dignified in every way. ³ This is good, and it is pleasing in the sight of God our Savior, ⁴ who desires all people to be saved and to come to the knowledge of the truth.

2 PETER 3:9

⁹ The Lord is not slow to fulfill his promise as some count slowness, but is patient toward you, not wishing that any should perish, but that all should reach repentance.

QUESTION 9: Why might these verses pose a problem for the five points of Calvinism? Articulate the tension created by these verses.

QUESTION 10: Think carefully about these two passages and about all of the other passages that you have examined. What are some possible ways to resolve the tension between 1 Timothy 2:4 and the doctrine of unconditional election?

FURTHER UP AND FURTHER IN

Read or listen to "The Freedom and Justice of God in Unconditional Election," an online sermon at the Desiring God Web site.

QUESTION 11: What objection does Paul raise in Romans 9:14? Where does this objection come from?

QUESTION 12: How does Paul respond to this objection? Why is Paul's answer to the objection puzzling to us? How does John Piper unpack Paul's response?

Read "Are There Two Wills in God? Divine Election and God's Desire for All to Be Saved," an online article at the Desiring God Web site.

QUESTION 13: Describe the difference between the two wills of God. Which biblical illustration of the two wills was most helpful to you?

QUESTION 14: John Piper argues that both Calvinists and Arminians affirm two wills in God. In the Arminian view, what is God's highest will? What is God's highest will according to the Calvinists?

QUESTION 15: Explain in your own words God's two "lenses." How does this help us to understand the two wills of God?

WHILE YOU WATCH THE DVD, TAKE NOTES

What is the key issue that John Piper is seeking to address from Romans 9?

What answer does John Piper find in Exodus 33:18–19?

How does John Piper define God's righteousness/justice?

What key concession does I. Howard Marshall make?

What do Calvinists and Arminians agree upon with respect to 1 Timothy 2:4?

AFTER YOU WATCH THE DVD, DISCUSS WHAT YOU'VE LEARNED

1) Discuss the flow of thought in Romans 9. Does John Piper's explanation do justice to the passage? What remaining questions do you have?

2) Piper defines God's justice as his "unswerving allegiance to always display and uphold his glory." How does unconditional election uphold God's glory?

3) Does God desire all men to be saved? Explain your answer using the two wills of God. What is the key difference between Calvinists and Arminians on this point?

AFTER YOU DISCUSS, MAKE APPLICATION

1) What was the most meaningful part of this lesson for you? Was there a sentence, concept, or idea that really struck you? Why? Record your thoughts in the space below.

2) When you consider that God chose you to be saved "before you were born or had done anything good or bad," what is your reaction? Meditate on the reality that your salvation is ultimately dependent upon the sovereign and unconditional mercy and freedom of God. Record your reflections below.

LESSON 12
LIMITED ATONEMENT: WHY DID JESUS NEED TO DIE?
A Companion Study to the TULIP DVD, Session 12

LESSON OBJECTIVES

It is our prayer that after you have finished this lesson . . .

> ❯ You will understand two key questions that we must ask about the atonement.
> ❯ You will grasp why the atonement of Christ was necessary.
> ❯ You will see how the cross of Christ solves a huge theological problem for God.

BEFORE YOU WATCH THE DVD, STUDY AND PREPARE

DAY 1: ASKING THE RIGHT QUESTIONS ABOUT THE ATONEMENT

In this lesson we begin our study of the doctrine of limited atonement. All Christians believe that Christ died for us. But Christians differ over the meaning of this phrase. In order to understand the atoning work of Christ, we must be sure and ask the right questions. The two questions that we will address are as follows:

> *What* did Christ accomplish in his death?
> *For whom* did he accomplish it?

We will explore the first question in this lesson and then take up the second in Lesson 13.

QUESTION 1: Look carefully at the questions given above. How would you answer these questions? Be sure to answer them carefully and with precision.

QUESTION 2: Why was the atonement of Christ necessary? Why did Christ need to die? Cite Scripture in your answer.

DAY 2: THE "WHY" OF THE ATONEMENT

As we begin to determine from the Bible *what* Christ accomplished in his death, we must first ask the question, "*Why* did he need to die in the first place?" Perhaps the most important passage in the Bible that addresses this question is Romans 3:21–26.

Study Romans 3:21–26.

ROMANS 3:21–26

> [21] *But now the righteousness of God has been manifested apart from the law, although the Law and the Prophets bear witness to it—* [22] *the righteousness of God through faith in Jesus Christ for all who believe. For there is no distinction:* [23] *for all have sinned and fall short of the glory of God,* [24] *and are justified by his grace as a gift, through the redemption that is in Christ Jesus,* [25] *whom God put forward as a propitiation by his blood, to be received by faith. This was to show God's righteousness, because in his divine forbearance he had passed over former sins.* [26] *It was to show his righteousness at the present time, so that he might be just and the justifier of the one who has faith in Jesus.*

QUESTION 3: This passage refers to the demonstration of God's righteousness (verses 21, 25–26). According to this passage, why did God need to demonstrate his righteousness? Explain your answer. (If necessary, refer back to John Piper's definition of righteousness in the previous lesson).

QUESTION 4: How does God demonstrate his righteousness in this passage? What does this demonstration enable God to do?

At the end of verse 26, Paul shows what God's two great goals were in the death of Jesus. Why did Jesus die? It was "so that [God] would be just and the justifier of the one who has faith in Jesus." To be righteous, and to reckon as righteous those who don't have their own righteousness. These seem to contradict each other. God's righteousness would dictate: pour out your wrath on sinners who exchange your glory for other values—that would be righteous. Or: have no wrath against the ungodly—that would be unrighteous. But if God wills that he demonstrate the infinite value of his glory and that he justify the ungodly, then someone—namely, Jesus Christ—had to bear the wrath of God to show that God does not take lightly the scorning of his glory. That's why the word "propitiation" in verse 25 is so important. Christ bore the wrath of God for our sins, and turned it away from us.[1]

DAY 3: CHRIST IN OUR PLACE

Reflect upon 2 Corinthians 5:21.

2 CORINTHIANS 5:21

21 For our sake he made him to be sin who knew no sin, so that in him we might become the righteousness of God.

QUESTION 5: Describe how the atonement works in this verse. What does Christ do? What is the result for us?

Look closely at 1 Peter 3:18.

1 PETER 3:18

[18] *For Christ also suffered once for sins, the righteous for the unrighteous, that he might bring us to God . . .*

QUESTION 6: How does the atonement work in this verse? What is the goal and purpose of the atonement?

DAY 4: GRACIOUSLY GIVEN ALL THINGS

One of the central passages that we have examined in this study guide is Romans 8:28–30. In it, we discovered key aspects of the doctrine of irresistible grace and the doctrine of unconditional election. We will now look at the verses following this passage in order to understand the atonement.

ROMANS 8:31–34

[31] *What then shall we say to these things? If God is for us, who can be against us?* [32] *He who did not spare his own Son but gave him up for us all, how will he not also with him graciously give us all things?* [33] *Who shall bring any charge against God's elect? It is God who justifies.* [34] *Who is to condemn? Christ Jesus is the one who died—more than that, who was raised—who is at the right hand of God, who indeed is interceding for us.*

QUESTION 7: Underline every reference to the death of Jesus in this passage. What great achievements did Christ accomplish for us in his death and resurrection?

QUESTION 8: Look closely at Romans 8:32. What is the central argument of this verse? How does the first half of the sentence relate to the second half of the sentence? What, then, is the key point that Paul is trying to communicate?

DAY 5: SUMMARIZING THE ACCOMPLISHMENT OF THE CROSS

As we close this lesson, it will be helpful to look at the BBC Elder Affirmation of Faith on The Saving Work of Christ.

> **THE SAVING WORK OF CHRIST**
> 7.1 We believe that by His perfect obedience to God and by His suffering and death as the immaculate Lamb of God, Jesus Christ obtained forgiveness of sins and the gift of perfect righteousness for all who trusted in Christ prior the cross and all who would trust in Christ thereafter. Through living a perfect life and dying in our place, the just for the unjust, Christ absorbed our punishment, appeased the wrath of God against us, vindicated the righteousness of God in our justification, and removed the condemnation of the law against us.

QUESTION 9: What did Christ accomplish for us on the cross? Underline every accomplishment of the cross in this passage. If you know of any other key passages that refer to the accomplishment of the cross, list them below.

QUESTION 10: As you look carefully at the BBC Elder Affirmation of Faith and at the biblical passages in this lesson, which of the following do you believe is more accurate?

A) The cross of Christ makes salvation possible.
B) The cross of Christ makes salvation certain.

Explain your answer.

FURTHER UP AND FURTHER IN

Read or listen to "The Demonstration of God's Righteousness, Part 3," an online sermon at the Desiring God Web site.

QUESTION 11: Why is the forgiveness of sins such a huge problem for God? How does John Piper illustrate this problem from the Old Testament? Why does the secular mind-set never wrestle with this problem?

QUESTION 12: How does the cross solve the problem created by the forgiveness of sins?

Read or listen to "God Did Not Spare His Own Son," an online sermon at the Desiring God Web site.

QUESTION 13: What are the possible answers to Paul's question in Romans 8:31? Why is the answer to this question complicated?

QUESTION 14: What does John Piper mean by the "solid logic of heaven"? Why is this logic so important for the Christian life? How does it provide a sure foundation for our salvation and our hope for the future?

QUESTION 15: Question 10 in this lesson asked whether the cross of Christ makes salvation possible or certain. Why do you think this question is so important to ask as we wrestle through limited atonement? What is the question seeking to determine?

WHILE YOU WATCH THE DVD, TAKE NOTES

Is the death and resurrection of Jesus the goal of history or a means to the goal?

Christ _____ for _____, but not for _____ in the _____ _____.

What does the word "propitiation" mean?

What is the dual commitment of God in the atonement?

What is the central argument of Romans 8:32?

AFTER YOU WATCH THE DVD, DISCUSS WHAT YOU'VE LEARNED

1) Why is the passing over of sins a huge theological problem for God? How does the cross address this problem?

2) What other important verses on the cross do you know? Share them with the group. How do they relate to what you have learned in this lesson?

3) Why is it important to reflect on whether the cross makes salvation possible or certain?

AFTER YOU DISCUSS, MAKE APPLICATION

1) What was the most meaningful part of this lesson for you? Was there a sentence, concept, or idea that really struck you? Why? Record your thoughts in the space below.

2) Memorize one of the passages on the cross that you studied in this lesson. Use that verse in your prayers this week. After memorizing this verse, seek an opportunity to share it with someone this week. Pray that God would provide the opportunity to do so.

NOTES

1. John Piper, "The Demonstration of God's Righteousness, Part 3," an online sermon at the Desiring God Web site.

LESSON 13
LIMITED ATONEMENT: WHO LIMITS THE ATONEMENT?
A Companion Study to the TULIP DVD, Session 13

LESSON OBJECTIVES

It is our prayer that after you have finished this lesson . . .

> You will gladly embrace the biblical truth that Christ secured the salvation of his people.

> You will grasp a way to honor both the universal and the particular texts on the atonement in Scripture.

> You will see how limited atonement gives great confidence to world missions.

BEFORE YOU WATCH THE DVD, STUDY AND PREPARE

DAY 1: THE PROBLEM OF LABELS

As we noted in the last lesson, we are seeking to determine the meaning of the phrase "Christ died for us." In the last lesson, we sought to answer the question, "What did Christ accomplish in his death?" In this lesson, we will address the second of the key questions: "For whom did he accomplish it?"

Before we examine the biblical material, we must first make a point about the use of labels.

QUESTION 1: Examine the following two sets of options. Circle the one in each set that you believe *sounds* more biblical. If you presented each set of terms to a group of Christians who were unfamiliar with the debate between Calvinists and Arminians, which options do you think they would identify as accurately representing biblical truth?

A) Limited Atonement vs. Unlimited Atonement

B) Definite Atonement vs. Indefinite Atonement

Many Christians would probably identify "Unlimited Atonement" as a more accurate label for the biblical teaching than "Limited Atonement." However, many of these same Christians would choose "Definite Atonement" over "Indefinite Atonement." The irony is that Definite Atonement is simply another description of Limited Atonement. The point of drawing attention to this fact is to seek to get beyond labels and to understand the substance of the biblical teaching. Far more important than the label is the doctrine itself.

QUESTION 2: Interact with the following statement: "*Both* Calvinists *and* Arminians limit the atonement." This will be a central argument later in the lesson. For now, what do you think this statement means? How do Calvinists limit the atonement? How do Arminians?

DAY 2: DETERMINING YOUR CURRENT VIEW

As we begin our study, it may be helpful to assess your current views on the extent of the atonement.

QUESTION 3: Which of the following statements accurately reflect your understanding of the atonement? (Circle all that apply).

A) Christ died to secure the salvation of his people.

B) Christ died to make salvation possible for all people.

C) Christ died to purchase the grace of the New Covenant.

D) Christ's death is sufficient for all people.

E) Christ's death is effective only for the elect.

No doubt one of the most beloved passages in the Bible is John 3:16.

JOHN 3:16

> ¹⁶ *For God so loved the world, that he gave his only Son, that whoever believes in him should not perish but have eternal life.*

QUESTION 4: Rewrite John 3:16 in your own words. In your view, is John 3:16 compatible with this statement: "Christ died to infallibly secure the salvation of his elect"?

DAY 3: FOR WHOM DID CHRIST DIE?

Study Ephesians 5:25–27 and John 10:14–15.

EPHESIANS 5:25–27

> [4] *Husbands, love your wives, as Christ loved the church and gave himself up for her,* [26] *that he might sanctify her, having cleansed her by the washing of water with the word,* [27] *so that he might present the church to himself in splendor, without spot or wrinkle or any such thing, that she might be holy and without blemish.*

JOHN 10:14–15

> [14] *I am the good shepherd. I know my own and my own know me,* [15] *just as the Father knows me and I know the Father; and I lay down my life for the sheep.*

QUESTION 5: In these verses, for whom did Christ die? Does his death make salvation possible or certain? Do these verses teach a limited or an unlimited atonement?

Study Romans 5:6–10.

ROMANS 5:6–10

> [6] *For while we were still weak, at the right time Christ died for the ungodly.* [7] *For one will scarcely die for a righteous person—*

though perhaps for a good person one would dare even to die—[8]
but God shows his love for us in that while we were still sinners,
Christ died for us. [9] *Since, therefore, we have now been justi-*
fied by his blood, much more shall we be saved by him from the
wrath of God. [10] *For if while we were enemies we were recon-*
ciled to God by the death of his Son, much more, now that we
are reconciled, shall we be saved by his life.

QUESTION 6: Underline every reference to the death of
Christ in this passage. Circle every reference to the people for
whom Christ died. Who is "we/us" in this passage? Does it refer
to all people or only to believers?

DAY 4: WHERE DOES THE GRACE OF THE NEW COVENANT COME FROM?

In previous lessons, we examined the promises of the new covenant. These promises were made in the Old Testament. Ezekiel
36:26–27 is one of the key new covenant promises. "And I will
give you a new heart, and a new spirit I will put within you. And
I will remove the heart of stone from your flesh and give you a
heart of flesh. And I will put my Spirit within you, and cause you
to walk in my statutes and be careful to obey my rules." In those
earlier lessons, we used these passages as evidence for the doctrine
of irresistible grace. But where does this grace come from?
Study Luke 22:19–20.

LUKE 22:19–20

> [19] *And he took bread, and when he had given thanks, he broke it and gave it to them, saying, "This is my body, which is given for you. Do this in remembrance of me."* [20] *And likewise the cup after they had eaten, saying, "This cup that is poured out for you is the new covenant in my blood."*

QUESTION 7: Does the new covenant passage in Ezekiel contain promises or commands? Where does the grace of the new covenant come from? Do all people receive the grace of the new covenant?

Thus far, we have examined passages that seem to imply a limited atonement. Christ died for his bride, the church, for his sheep, for those who are justified and reconciled to God. For them, he purchases the irresistible grace of the new covenant. For these reasons, we argue that the atonement is in some sense limited.

But what about other passages which seem to indicate an unlimited and universal atonement?

Look carefully at 1 Timothy 2:1–6 and 1 John 2:2.

1 TIMOTHY 2:1–6

> [1] *First of all, then, I urge that supplications, prayers, intercessions, and thanksgivings be made for all people,* [2] *for kings and all who are in high positions, that we may lead a peaceful and quiet life, godly and dignified in every way.* [3] *This is good, and it is pleasing in the sight of God our Savior,* [4] *who desires all*

people to be saved and to come to the knowledge of the truth.
⁵ For there is one God, and there is one mediator between God
and men, the man Christ Jesus, ⁶ who gave himself as a ransom
for all, which is the testimony given at the proper time.

1 JOHN 2:2

² He is the propitiation for our sins, and not for ours only but
also for the sins of the whole world.

QUESTION 8: Do these passages teach a completely universal atonement? Does the fact that Christ is "a ransom for all" mean that all will be saved?

DAY 5: WHAT DID CHRIST PURCHASE?

In the book of Revelation, there is a magnificent scene in which the Lion of the Tribe of Judah, the Lamb of God, takes the scroll of history in order to open it and reveal its contents. When he takes the scroll, the four living creatures and the twenty-four elders fall down and worship the Lamb.

Reflect upon Revelation 5:9–10.

REVELATION 5:9–10

⁹ And they sang a new song, saying, "Worthy are you to take
the scroll and to open its seals, for you were slain, and by your
blood you ransomed people for God from every tribe and
language and people and nation, ¹⁰ and you have made them
a kingdom and priests to our God, and they shall reign on the
earth."

QUESTION 9: In this passage, what does Jesus ransom or purchase? Is it salvation or is it people? Is this a potential ransom of people or an actual ransom of people? Do all those who are bought by Christ with his blood become a kingdom and priests to God?

Look once more at Romans 8:28–32.

ROMANS 8:28–32

> [28] And we know that for those who love God all things work together for good, for those who are called according to his purpose. [29] For those whom he foreknew he also predestined to be conformed to the image of his Son, in order that he might be the firstborn among many brothers. [30] And those whom he predestined he also called, and those whom he called he also justified, and those whom he justified he also glorified. [31] What then shall we say to these things? If God is for us, who can be against us? [32] He who did not spare his own Son but gave him up for us all, how will he not also with him graciously give us all things?

QUESTION 10: Look closely at Romans 8:32. Keeping the entire context of this passage in mind, what do you think is included in "all things"? In light of this, who is included in the "us all" of verse 32?

FURTHER UP AND FURTHER IN

Read or listen to "For Whom Did Jesus Taste Death?," an online sermon at the Desiring God Web site.

QUESTION 11: What does John Piper think about those who believe that Jesus tasted death for everyone?

QUESTION 12: What question does John Piper pose to those who believe that Jesus died for everyone in the same way? What problem is created by this viewpoint?

QUESTION 13: To whom does the word "everyone" refer in Hebrews 2:9? Are you persuaded by John Piper's explanation?

Read the Limited Atonement section of "What We Believe about the Five Points of Calvinism," an online article at the Desiring God Web site.

QUESTION 14: Does limited atonement deny that all men are the beneficiaries of the atonement in some way? What benefits do all men receive from the atonement in the Calvinistic view?

QUESTION 15: What additional truth did you learn from reading this explanation that you did not learn in the preparatory study or the DVD session?

WHILE YOU WATCH THE DVD, TAKE NOTES

Arminians limit the _____ of the atonement by _____ that it _____ the promises of the _____ _____ for _____ _____.

Calvinists limit the _____ _____ of the atonement to those God _____ _____ to _____.

What do Arminians mean by "Christ died for you"?

What "more" does the Calvinist believe?

How does John Piper use his love for his wife to illustrate the love of God in the atonement?

AFTER YOU WATCH THE DVD, DISCUSS WHAT YOU'VE LEARNED

1) This lesson has argued that both Calvinists and Arminians limit the atonement. Having heard this argument, do you agree with it? What questions do you still have about the limitations of the atonement?

2) What is the heart of the disagreement between Calvinists and Arminians? Is it possible to believe that Christ died to make salvation *possible* for *all* people (unlimited atonement) and yet still believe that he died to make salvation *certain* for the *elect* (limited atonement)?

3) How does John Piper demonstrate that Christ purchased irresistible grace for the elect? Do you find his
   argument convincing? Explain your answer.

AFTER YOU DISCUSS, MAKE APPLICATION

1) What was the most meaningful part of this lesson for you?
   Was there a sentence, concept, or idea that really struck
   you? Why? Record your thoughts in the space below.

2) One of the applications of this lesson is that it is possible to give a genuine offer of the gospel to every
   person on the planet because Christ has purchased this
   offer for them. This lesson also teaches that we can
   have confidence that some will respond to the message
   of the cross because Christ has purchased irresistible
   grace for them on the cross. Spend some time praying
   for opportunities to share the gospel with someone this
   week. Review the central truths of the gospel so that
   you are ready when God answers this prayer. Record
   any reflections you have in the space below.

LESSON 14
PERSEVERANCE OF THE SAINTS: THE NECESSITY OF ENDURANCE
A Companion Study to the TULIP DVD, Session 14

LESSON OBJECTIVES

It is our prayer that after you have finished this lesson . . .

> ❯ You will embrace the truth that perseverance in faith is necessary for final salvation.

> ❯ You will begin to think through how to use this doctrine in practical situations.

> ❯ You will understand what evidence must be present in order to confirm that a person is saved.

BEFORE YOU WATCH THE DVD, STUDY AND PREPARE

DAY 1: IS PERSEVERANCE NECESSARY?

We come now to the final doctrine that we will examine: the perseverance of the saints. This lesson will seek to determine whether or not perseverance is necessary if we are to be saved on the last day. We begin with a hypothetical situation.

You discover that Bob, a man at your church, has been committing adultery on his wife for the past two years. Bob is a professing Christian, but, when confronted with his sin, he defends himself and refuses to repent. He plans to leave his wife and two children and start a new life with his mistress.

QUESTION 1: Which of the following statements are you likely to say to Bob? (Circle all that apply.)

A) "Bob, you're definitely going to hell."

B) "Bob, if you don't repent, then you will not be saved when Jesus returns."

C) "Bob, I believe that you are a Christian and that your eternal salvation is secure, but if you continue in this sin, you will lose rewards in heaven."

D) "Bob, I believe that you were a Christian. But this unrepentant sin means that you have lost your salvation. You need to repent and believe in Jesus in order to be re-saved."

E) Other: _____

QUESTION 2: Interact with the following statement: "Lifelong perseverance in faith is the necessary evidence that we have been saved. If we fail to persevere in faith, we will not enter the kingdom."

DAY 2: PERSEVERANCE OR ETERNAL SECURITY?

Carefully read the BBC Elder Affirmation of Faith on God's Work in Sanctification.

GOD'S WORK IN FAITH AND SANCTIFICATION

10.3 We believe that this persevering, future-oriented, Christ-embracing, heart-satisfying faith is life-transforming, and therefore renders intelligible the teaching of the Scripture that final salvation in the age to come depends on the transformation of life, and yet does not contradict justification by faith alone. The faith which alone justifies, cannot remain alone, but works through love . . .

10.5 We believe that sanctification, which comes by the Spirit through faith, is imperfect and incomplete in this life. Although slavery to sin is broken, and sinful desires are progressively weakened by the power of a superior satisfaction in the glory of Christ, yet there remain remnants of corruption in every heart that give rise to irreconcilable war, and call for vigilance in the lifelong fight of faith.

QUESTION 3: What important truths are taught in these two paragraphs? What questions are prompted as you read it? Why are both paragraphs important?

At times, the doctrine of the perseverance of the saints is called "eternal security." However, it is not always clear that advocates of eternal security and advocates of perseverance of the saints hold to the exact same doctrine.

QUESTION 4: What differences might there be between perseverance of the saints and eternal security? What are the different emphases in the names of these two doctrines?

DAY 3: BELIEVING IN VAIN

This study guide will argue that perseverance in faith is necessary if we are to be saved. Many biblical texts teach this truth.

Read 1 Corinthians 15:1–2.

1 CORINTHIANS 15:1–2

> [1] *Now I would remind you, brothers, of the gospel I preached to you, which you received, in which you stand,* [2] *and by which you are being saved, if you hold fast to the word I preached to you—unless you believed in vain.*

QUESTION 5: What do you think "believed in vain" means in this passage? How can we be sure that we have not "believed in vain"?

The tense of the verb "believe" here is crucial. It signi-
fies ongoing action, not just the first act of faith when
you were converted: "The gospel . . . is the power of God
unto salvation to everyone who is believing"—who goes
on believing. It's the same as 1 Corinthians 15:1–2 where
Paul says, "I preached to you [the gospel], which also you
received, in which also you stand, by which also you are
being saved, if you hold fast the word which I preached
to you, unless you believed in vain." Faith that does not
persevere is a vain and empty faith—what James calls
"dead faith" (James 2:17, 26).[1]

Study Colossians 1:21–23.

COLOSSIANS 1:21–23

²¹ *And you, who once were alienated and hostile in mind, doing evil deeds,* ²² *he has now reconciled in his body of flesh by his death, in order to present you holy and blameless and above reproach before him,* ²³ *if indeed you continue in the faith, stable and steadfast, not shifting from the hope of the gospel that you heard, which has been proclaimed in all creation under heaven, and of which I, Paul, became a minister.*

QUESTION 6: What is the key condition that must be met if we are to be presented holy and blameless before God on the last day? Underline the relevant phrases. What is your reaction to a verse like this?

DAY 4: WHO WILL NOT INHERIT THE KINGDOM?

We continue our examination of the necessity of perseverance in faith by looking at two passages that refer to our final salvation.

Study Hebrews 12:14 and Romans 8:13.

HEBREWS 12:14

14 *Strive for peace with everyone, and for the holiness without which no one will see the Lord.*

ROMANS 8:13

13 *For if you live according to the flesh you will die, but if by the Spirit you put to death the deeds of the body, you will live.*

QUESTION 7: Underline every phrase that teaches that we must persevere in faith. What is necessary if we are to see the Lord and live? Does this mean that we must be flawlessly perfect?

Paul often issued dire warnings to people in his churches about the dangers of persistent sin.

Study Galatians 5:19–21 and 1 Corinthians 6:9–10.

GALATIANS 5:19–21

19 *Now the works of the flesh are evident: sexual immorality, impurity, sensuality,* 20 *idolatry, sorcery, enmity, strife, jealousy,*

fits of anger, rivalries, dissensions, divisions, ²¹ envy, drunken-
ness, orgies, and things like these. I warn you, as I warned
you before, that those who do such things will not inherit the
kingdom of God.

1 CORINTHIANS 6:9–10

⁹ Do you not know that the unrighteous will not inherit the
kingdom of God? Do not be deceived: neither the sexually
immoral, nor idolaters, nor adulterers, nor men who practice
homosexuality, ¹⁰ nor thieves, nor the greedy, nor drunkards,
nor revilers, nor swindlers will inherit the kingdom of God.

QUESTION 8: What is the result for those who practice the
works of the flesh? Why do you think Paul tells the Corinthians,
"Do not be deceived"? What deception is he talking about? What
is your reaction to passages like this?

I do not mean that our faith produces a *perfect flawlessness*
in this life. I mean that it produces a *persevering fight.*[2]

DAY 5: THE SHOCKING WORDS OF JESUS AND JOHN

Jesus was not afraid to use shocking words to describe the necessity of perseverance.

Study Matthew 5:27–30 and Matthew 6:14–15.

MATTHEW 5:27–30

27 You have heard that it was said, "You shall not commit adultery." 28 But I say to you that everyone who looks at a woman with lustful intent has already committed adultery with her in his heart. 29 If your right eye causes you to sin, tear it out and throw it away. For it is better that you lose one of your members than that your whole body be thrown into hell. 30 And if your right hand causes you to sin, cut it off and throw it away. For it is better that you lose one of your members than that your whole body go into hell.

MATTHEW 6:14–15

14 For if you forgive others their trespasses, your heavenly Father will also forgive you, 15 but if you do not forgive others their trespasses, neither will your Father forgive your trespasses.

QUESTION 9: What are the consequences if we fail to make war on our sin or if we fail to forgive others? What does this teach us about the necessity of perseverance?

The book of 1 John emphasizes tests of genuineness to determine if we are truly born again.

Study 1 John 2:3–6; 3:6–10; 3:14; and 4:20.

1 JOHN 2:3–6

3 And by this we know that we have come to know him, if we keep his commandments. 4 Whoever says "I know him" but does not keep his commandments is a liar, and the truth is not in him, 5 but whoever keeps his word, in him truly the love of God is perfected. By this we may know that we are in him: 6 whoever says he abides in him ought to walk in the same way in which he walked.

1 JOHN 3:6–10

> [6] No one who abides in him keeps on sinning; no one who keeps on sinning has either seen him or known him. [7] Little children, let no one deceive you. Whoever practices righteousness is righteous, as he is righteous. [8] Whoever makes a practice of sinning is of the devil, for the devil has been sinning from the beginning. The reason the Son of God appeared was to destroy the works of the devil. [9] No one born of God makes a practice of sinning, for God's seed abides in him, and he cannot keep on sinning because he has been born of God. [10] By this it is evident who are the children of God, and who are the children of the devil: whoever does not practice righteousness is not of God, nor is the one who does not love his brother.

1 JOHN 3:14

> [14] We know that we have passed out of death into life, because we love the brothers. Whoever does not love abides in death.

1 JOHN 4:20

> [20] If anyone says, "I love God," and hates his brother, he is a liar; for he who does not love his brother whom he has seen cannot love God whom he has not seen.

QUESTION 10: Summarize the teaching of these passages in your own words. What is the necessary evidence that we have been born again and saved?

FURTHER UP AND FURTHER IN

Read or listen to "The Doctrine of Perseverance: The Future of a Fruitless Field," an online sermon at the Desiring God Web site.

QUESTION 11: What is at stake in the fight of faith? How does Piper prove this point from the book of Hebrews?

QUESTION 12: What does it mean to "fall away"?

Read the Perseverance of the Saints section in "What We Believe about the Five Points of Calvinism," an online article at the Desiring God Web site.

QUESTION 13: Does the call to persevere mean that we must be perfect? How do we know?

QUESTION 14: How do we reconcile the doctrine of justification by faith with the doctrine of perseverance of the saints?

Read the Concluding Testimonies section in "What We Believe about the Five Points of Calvinism," an online article at the Desiring God web site.

QUESTION 15: Which historical testimony was most encouraging to you?

WHILE YOU WATCH THE DVD, TAKE NOTES

According to John Piper, why did you wake up a Christian this morning?

What is the main point of 1 Corinthians 15:1–2?

According to John Piper, what is the key difference between perseverance and eternal security?

How did John Piper use the doctrine of perseverance in practical ministry?

_____ the brethren is a _____ _____ that you have been _____ _____.

AFTER YOU WATCH THE DVD, DISCUSS WHAT YOU'VE LEARNED

1) Think about the difference between the doctrine of perseverance of the saints and the doctrine of automatic, mechanical, eternal security. Why do you think it is important to emphasize that we must persevere? What practical difference does it make in your life?

2) How does John Piper address professing Christians living in unrepentant sin? How does this compare to your answer to Question 1 in this lesson? Would you modify your approach after completing this lesson?

3) How can we reconcile the biblical truth that we must persevere in order to be saved with the doctrine of justification by faith alone?

AFTER YOU DISCUSS, MAKE APPLICATION

1) What was the most meaningful part of this lesson for you? Was there a sentence, concept, or idea that really struck you? Why? Record your thoughts in the space below.

2) Spend some time reflecting on your own struggle with sin. Are there any areas in your life where you have grown complacent? How has this lesson changed the way that you view the fight against sin? Record your reflections on your personal sanctification in the space below.

NOTES

1. John Piper, "The Gospel Is the Power of God unto Salvation," an online sermon at the Desiring God Web site.
2. John Piper, *Future Grace* (Sisters, Oregon: Multnomah, 2003), 332.

LESSON 15
PERSEVERANCE OF THE SAINTS: KEPT BY THE POWER OF GOD
A Companion Study to the TULIP DVD, Session 15

LESSON OBJECTIVES

It is our prayer that after you have finished this lesson . . .

- › You will grasp the relationship between our perseverance and God's preservation.
- › You will grow in the sovereign, sustaining grace of Christ.
- › You will understand how we should regard those who fall away.

BEFORE YOU WATCH THE DVD, STUDY AND PREPARE

DAY 1: PERSEVERING IN FAITH, PRESERVED BY GOD

In the last lesson, we saw that perseverance in faith is necessary for final salvation and is the necessary evidence that we have been born again. This is an important truth and one that is sorely lack-

186

ing in many churches. However, the necessity of our perseverance is not the whole story; God also preserves and keeps us in the faith.

Meditate on 1 Peter 1:3–5.

1 PETER 1:3–5

3 *Blessed be the God and Father of our Lord Jesus Christ! According to his great mercy, he has caused us to be born again to a living hope through the resurrection of Jesus Christ from the dead,* 4 *to an inheritance that is imperishable, undefiled, and unfading, kept in heaven for you,* 5 *who by God's power are being guarded through faith for a salvation ready to be revealed in the last time.*

QUESTION 1: Underline the reference to our perseverance in this passage. Circle the reference to God's preservation of us. How does this passage help us to emphasize both God's work and our work?

Consider Jude 1:24–25.

JUDE 1:24–25

24 *Now to him who is able to keep you from stumbling and to present you blameless before the presence of his glory with great joy,* 25 *to the only God, our Savior, through Jesus Christ our Lord, be glory, majesty, dominion, and authority, before all time and now and forever. Amen.*

QUESTION 2: How can we have confidence that we won't stumble and fall away from Christ? How does this verse encourage those who aren't sure whether they will persevere to the end?

DAY 2: THOSE WHOM HE JUSTIFIED HE GLORIFIED

Throughout this study guide, we have looked at Romans 8:28–30. We return to this passage one last time.

Look again at Romans 8:28–30.

ROMANS 8:28–30

> [28] And we know that for those who love God all things work together for good, for those who are called according to his purpose. [29] For those whom he foreknew he also predestined to be conformed to the image of his Son, in order that he might be the firstborn among many brothers. [30] And those whom he predestined he also called, and those whom he called he also justified, and those whom he justified he also glorified.

QUESTION 3: Romans 8:29–30 is often called the "golden chain of redemption." Does anyone drop out of this "golden chain"? How do you know?

Study John 10:25–30.

JOHN 10:25–30

> ²⁵ *Jesus answered them, "I told you, and you do not believe. The works that I do in my Father's name bear witness about me,* ²⁶ *but you do not believe because you are not part of my flock.* ²⁷ *My sheep hear my voice, and I know them, and they follow me.* ²⁸ *I give them eternal life, and they will never perish, and no one will snatch them out of my hand.* ²⁹ *My Father, who has given them to me, is greater than all, and no one is able to snatch them out of the Father's hand.* ³⁰ *I and the Father are one."*

QUESTION 4: How do you see the necessity of our perseverance in this passage? Where do you see the promise of God's preservation?

DAY 3: GOD'S EVERLASTING COVENANT

In earlier lessons, we looked at the promises of the new covenant. One of the greatest new covenant promises is found in Jeremiah 32:40.

Read Jeremiah 32:40.

JEREMIAH 32:40

> *I will make with them an everlasting covenant, that I will not turn away from doing good to them. And I will put the fear of me in their hearts, that they may not turn from me.*

QUESTION 5: What are the two promises that God makes in this verse? How can we be sure that God will not turn from us? How can we be sure that we will not turn from God?

> God promises that he will not turn away from us and we will not turn away from him. Verse 40: "I will make an everlasting covenant with them that I will not turn away from them, to do them good; and I will put the fear of Me in their hearts so that they will not turn away from Me." In other words, his heart work is so powerful that he guarantees we will not turn from him. This is what's new about the new covenant: God promises to fulfill by his power the conditions that we have to meet. We must fear him and love him and trust him. And he says, I will see to that. I will "put the fear of me in their hearts"—not to see what they will do with it, but in such a way that "they will not turn from me." This is sovereign, sustaining grace.[1]

Many of the New Testament letters contain doxologies. Doxologies are short prayers and blessings that often express what the writer wants God to do for the people to whom he is writing. Such doxologies offer us great comfort and encouragement.

Meditate upon Hebrews 13:20–21, 1 Thessalonians 5:23–24, and 2 Thessalonians 1:11–12.

HEBREWS 13:20–21

²⁰ *Now may the God of peace who brought again from the dead our Lord Jesus, the great shepherd of the sheep, by the blood of the eternal covenant,* ²¹ *equip you with everything good that you may do his will, working in us that which is pleasing in his sight, through Jesus Christ, to whom be glory forever and ever. Amen.*

1 THESSALONIANS 5:23–24

²³ *Now may the God of peace himself sanctify you completely, and may your whole spirit and soul and body be kept blameless at the coming of our Lord Jesus Christ.* ²⁴ *He who calls you is faithful; he will surely do it.*

2 THESSALONIANS 1:11–12

¹¹ *To this end we always pray for you, that our God may make you worthy of his calling and may fulfill every resolve for good and every work of faith by his power,* ¹² *so that the name of our Lord Jesus may be glorified in you, and you in him, according to the grace of our God and the Lord Jesus Christ.*

QUESTION 6: What common themes do you see in these three doxologies? Underline the phrases that refer to God's preserving power.

DAY 4: WHAT ABOUT THOSE WHO FALL AWAY?

No discussion of the perseverance of the saints would be complete without addressing the question of those who fall away. The Bible is full of examples of those who did not finish well. The obvious example is, of course, Judas, a member of the twelve disciples and Jesus' betrayer. Others, like Hymenaeus and Alexander, are said to have made "shipwreck of their faith" (1 Timothy 1:19–20). If we believe that the God who chose us, redeemed us with the blood of his Son, and irresistibly called us to himself will infallibly cause us to persevere, then how do we explain those who gave evidence of conversion and then fell away?

Look closely at 1 John 2:19

1 JOHN 2:19

> ¹⁹ *They went out from us, but they were not of us; for if they had been of us, they would have continued with us. But they went out, that it might become plain that they all are not of us.*

QUESTION 7: How does John regard those who went out from the believers? Did they lose their salvation? What did their leaving demonstrate?

Reflect upon Hebrews 3:12–14.

HEBREWS 3:12–14

> ¹² *Take care, brothers, lest there be in any of you an evil, unbelieving heart, leading you to fall away from the living God.* ¹³ *But exhort one another every day, as long as it is called "today," that none of you may be hardened by the deceitfulness*

of sin. [14] *For we have come to share in Christ, if indeed we hold our original confidence firm to the end.*

QUESTION 8: What warning and exhortation does Paul give in this passage? Using this passage, how would you respond to those who argue that we can lose our participation in Christ?

DAY 5: RESPONDING TO PERSEVERANCE OF THE SAINTS

We have seen that God promises to preserve his people. All those who are justified are glorified. No one drops out. However, this does not mean that we can be complacent, for God promises to guard us *through faith*, meaning that we must persevere in believing. If we fail to persevere, then we demonstrate that we were never truly partakers of Christ. Having seen all these things, what should our response be?

Look carefully at 2 Peter 1:10–11.

2 PETER 1:10–11

[10] *Therefore, brothers, be all the more diligent to make your calling and election sure, for if you practice these qualities you will never fall.* [11] *For in this way there will be richly provided for you an entrance into the eternal kingdom of our Lord and Savior Jesus Christ.*

QUESTION 9: What exhortation does Peter give to his readers in this passage? Why is the way that he phrases his exhortation important? How does it honor the various doctrines that we have been studying?

One of the most important texts in the Bible on the relationship between the sovereign activity of God and the responsible activity of man is found in the book of Philippians.

Carefully study Philippians 2:12–13.

PHILIPPIANS 2:12–13

> [12] *Therefore, my beloved, as you have always obeyed, so now, not only as in my presence but much more in my absence, work out your own salvation with fear and trembling,* [13] *for it is God who works in you, both to will and to work for his good pleasure.*

QUESTION 10: What is the logical relationship between verse 12 and verse 13? Why is the order important? What would happen if you reversed the logical relationship? How does this verse reflect the truths of God's preservation and our perseverance?

FURTHER UP AND FURTHER IN

Read or listen to "Eternal Security Is a Community Project," an online sermon at the Desiring God Web site.

QUESTION 11: What explanation does John Piper give for those who fall away? Were they ever saved?

QUESTION 12: Where does our assurance of salvation come from? How can we be confident that we will be saved on the last day?

QUESTION 13: What is the role of the church in securing our perseverance? What are some practical implications of this truth that you can apply to your own life?

Read or listen to "Sustained by Sovereign Grace Forever," an online sermon at the Desiring God Web site.

QUESTION 14: In what situations do we need sustaining grace? Of the ones given by John Piper, which one is most relevant to you right now?

QUESTION 15: How can we be sure of the triumph of grace? How should the triumph of grace affect the way that we pray? If we know that grace will triumph in our lives, why should we still pray?

WHILE YOU WATCH THE DVD, TAKE NOTES

What is written on the grave of John Piper's mother?

Our _____ comes not from _____ _____, but in _____ their _____.

What encouragement does John Piper draw from Satan's sifting of Peter?

_____ doesn't _____ you a _____. It _____ that you are one.

What language does John Piper recommend that we use to talk about our perseverance?

AFTER YOU WATCH THE DVD, DISCUSS WHAT YOU'VE LEARNED

1) Can a Christian lose his salvation? How do we explain Christians who fall away from the faith? Explain your answer.

2) John Piper notes that "eternal security is a community project." What do you think this statement means? What practical effects should it have on the way that we seek to persevere in faith? What errors should it lead us to avoid?

3) Why is this lesson a necessary counterpart to Lesson 14? Discuss what happens when Christians emphasize only our perseverance or only God's preservation.

AFTER YOU DISCUSS, MAKE APPLICATION

1) What was the most meaningful part of this lesson for you? Was there a sentence, concept, or idea that really struck you? Why? Record your thoughts in the space below.

2) In this lesson, you learned about doxologies (short prayers that express theological truth and call down blessing over yourself and others). Write your own short prayer using the material from the last two lessons. You are encouraged to use phrases and sentences from biblical passages. Seek to use this doxology in your prayers this week. Use it often enough that the truth in it becomes a core part of your theology and practice.

NOTES

1. John Piper, "Sustained by Sovereign Grace Forever," an online sermon at the Desiring God Web site.

LESSON 16
TEN EFFECTS OF BELIEVING THE FIVE POINTS OF CALVINISM
A Companion Study to the TULIP DVD, Session 16

LESSON OBJECTIVES

It is our prayer that after you have finished this lesson . . .

> You will be able to summarize and synthesize what you've learned.

> You will hear what others in your group have learned.

> You will begin to see some of the practical effects of embracing the five points of Calvinism.

WHAT HAVE YOU LEARNED?

There are no study questions to answer in preparation for this lesson. Instead, spend your time writing a few paragraphs that explain what you've learned in this group study. In particular, make note of any practical changes and effects that you have noticed in your life since you began this study. To help you do this, you may choose to review the notes you've taken in the previous lessons. Then, after you've written down what you've learned, write down some questions that still remain in your mind about anything addressed in these lessons. Be prepared to share these reflections and questions with the group in the next lesson.

NOTES

Use this space to record anything in the DVD session or in the group discussion that you want to remember.

LEADER'S GUIDE

AS THE LEADER OF THIS GROUP STUDY, *it is imperative that you are completely familiar with this study guide* and with the *TULIP* DVD set. Therefore, it is our strong recommendation that you (1) read and understand the introduction, (2) skim each lesson, surveying its layout and content, and (3) read the entire Leader's Guide *before* you begin the group study and distribute the study guides. As you review this Leader's Guide, keep in mind that the material here is only a recommendation. As the leader of the study, feel free to adapt this study guide to your situation and context.

BEFORE LESSON 1

Before the first lesson, you will need to know approximately how many participants you will have in your group study. *Each participant will need his or her own study guide!* Therefore, be sure to order enough study guides. You will distribute these study guides at the beginning of the first lesson.

It is also our strong recommendation that you, as the leader, familiarize yourself with this study guide and the *TULIP* DVD set in order to answer any questions that might arise and also to ensure that each group session runs smoothly and maximizes the learning of the participants. It is not necessary for you to preview *TULIP* in its entirety—although it certainly wouldn't hurt!—but you should be prepared to navigate your way through each DVD menu.

DURING LESSON 1

Each lesson is designed for a one-hour group session. Lessons 2–16 require preparatory work from the participant before this group session. Lesson 1, however, requires no preparation on the part of the participant.

The following schedule is how we suggest that you use the first hour of your group study:

INTRODUCTION TO THE STUDY GUIDE (5 MINUTES)

Introduce this study guide and the *TULIP* DVD. Share with the group why you chose to lead the group study using these resources. Inform your group of the commitment that this study will require and motivate them to work hard. Pray for the sixteen-week study, asking God for the grace you will need. Then distribute one study guide to each participant. You may read the introduction aloud, if you want, or you may immediately turn the group to Lesson 1 (starting on page 13 of this study guide).

PERSONAL INTRODUCTIONS (5 MINUTES)

Since group discussion will be an integral part of this guided study, it is crucial that each participant feels welcome and safe. The goal of each lesson is for every participant to contribute to the discussion in some way. Therefore, during these 5 minutes, have the participants introduce themselves. You may choose to use the questions listed in the section entitled, "About Yourself," or you may ask questions of your own choosing.

DVD VIEWING (40 MINUTES)

Play session 1 on the *TULIP* DVD. Because this session is long (approximately 40 minutes), you may want to schedule more time for the first class session. You will need to communicate this to your students before the class meets. Otherwise you will not have time for discussion.

DISCUSSION AND CLOSING (10 MINUTES)

Foster discussion on what was taught during John Piper's session. You may do this by first reviewing the DVD notes (under the heading "While You Watch the DVD, Take Notes") and then proceeding to the discussion questions, listed under the heading "After You Watch the DVD, Discuss What You've Learned." These discussion questions are meant to be springboards that launch the group into further and deeper discussion. Don't feel constrained to these questions if the group discussion begins to move in other helpful directions.

End the group session by reviewing Lesson 2 with the group participants and informing them of the preparation that they must do before the group meets again. Encourage them to be faithful in preparing for the next lesson. Answer any questions that the group may have and then close in prayer.

BEFORE LESSONS 2–15

As the group leader, you should do all the preparation for each lesson that is required of the group participants, that is, the ten study questions. Furthermore, it is highly recommended that you complete the entire "Further Up and Further In" section. This is not required of the group participants, but it will enrich your preparation and help you to guide and shape the conversation more effectively.

The group leader should also preview the session of *TULIP* that will be covered in the next lesson. So, for example, if the group participants are doing the preparatory work for Lesson 3, you should preview *TULIP*, Session 3, before the group meets and views it. Previewing each session will better equip you to understand the material and answer questions. If you want to pause the DVD in the midst of the session in order to clarify or discuss, previewing the session will allow you to plan where you want to take your pauses.

Finally, you may want to supplement or modify the discussion questions or the application assignment. Please remember that *this study guide is a resource*; any additions or changes you make that better match the study to your particular group are encouraged. As the group leader, your own discernment, creativity, and guidance are invaluable, and you should adapt the material as you see fit.

Plan for about two hours of your own preparation before each lesson!

DURING LESSONS 2–15

Again, let us stress that during Lessons 2–15, you may use the group time in whatever way you desire. The following schedule, however, is what we suggest:

DISCUSSION (10 MINUTES)

Begin your time with prayer. The tone you set in your prayer will likely be impressed upon the group participants: if your prayer is serious and heart-felt, the group participants will be serious about prayer; if your prayer is hasty, sloppy, or a token gesture, the group participants will share this same attitude toward prayer. So model the kind of praying that you desire your students to imitate. Remember, the blood of Jesus has bought your access to the throne of grace.

After praying, review the preparatory work that the participants completed. How did they answer the questions? Which questions did they find to be the most interesting or the most confusing? What observations or insights can they share with the group? If you would like to review some tips for leading productive discussion, please turn to the appendix at the end of this Leader's Guide.

The group participants will be provided an opportunity to apply what they've learned in Lessons 2–15. As the group leader, you can choose whether it would be appropriate for the group to discuss these assignments during this ten-minute time-slot.

DVD VIEWING (30 MINUTES)[1]

Play the session for TULIP that corresponds to the lesson you're studying. You may choose to pause the DVD at crucial points to check for understanding and provide clarification. Or you may choose to watch the DVD without interruption.

DISCUSSION AND CLOSING (20 MINUTES)

Foster discussion on what was taught during John Piper's session. You may do this by first reviewing the DVD notes (under the heading "While You Watch the DVD, Take Notes") and then proceeding to the discussion questions, listed under the heading "After You Watch the DVD, Discuss What You've Learned." These discussion questions are meant to be springboards that launch the group into further and deeper discussion. Don't feel constrained to cover these questions if the group discussion begins to move in other helpful directions.

Close the time by briefly reviewing the application section and the homework that is expected for the next lesson. Pray and dismiss.

BEFORE LESSON 16

It is important that you encourage the group participants to complete the preparatory work for Lesson 16. This assignment invites the participants to reflect on what they've learned and what remaining questions they still have. As the group leader, this would be a helpful assignment for you to complete as well. In addition, you may want to write down the key concepts of this DVD series that you want the group participants to walk away with.

DURING LESSON 16

The group participants are expected to complete a reflection exercise as part of their preparation for Lesson 16. You will also view the last session on the *TULIP* DVD. This session will focus on ten effects of believing the five points of Calvinism. It may provide springboards for your final discussion time. The bulk of the group time during this last lesson should be focused on reviewing and synthesizing what was learned. Encourage each participant to share some recorded thoughts. Attempt to answer any remaining questions that they might have.

To close this last lesson, you might want to spend extended time in prayer. If appropriate, take prayer requests relating to what the participants have learned in these sixteen weeks, and bring these requests to God.

It would be completely appropriate for you, the group leader, to give a final charge or word of exhortation to end this group study. Speak from your heart and out of the overflow of joy that you have in God.

Please receive our blessing for all of you group leaders who choose to use this study guide:

> The LORD bless you and keep you; the LORD make his face to shine upon you and be gracious to you; the LORD lift up his countenance upon you and give you peace. (Numbers 6:24–26)

NOTES

1. Thirty minutes is only an approximation. Some of the sessions are shorter; some are longer. You may need to budget your group time differently, depending upon which session you are viewing.

APPENDIX
LEADING PRODUCTIVE DISCUSSIONS

Note: This material has been adapted from curricula produced by The Bethlehem Institute (TBI), a ministry of Bethlehem Baptist Church. It is used by permission.

IT IS OUR CONVICTION THAT the best group leaders foster an environment in their group that engages the participants. Most people learn by solving problems or by working through things that provoke curiosity or concern. Therefore, we discourage you from ever "lecturing" for the entire lesson. Although a group leader will constantly shape conversation, clarifying and correcting as needed, they will probably not talk for the majority of the lesson. This study guide is meant to facilitate an investigation into biblical truth—an investigation that is shared by the group leader and the participants. Therefore, we encourage you to adopt the posture of a "fellow-learner" who invites participation from everyone in the group.

It might surprise you how eager people can be to share what they have learned in preparing for each lesson. Therefore, you should invite participation by asking your group participants to share their discoveries. Here are some of our "tips" on facilitating discussion that is engaging and helpful:

> › Don't be uncomfortable with silence initially. Once the first participant shares their response, others will be likely to join in. But if you cut the silence short by prompting them, then they are more likely to wait for you to prompt them every time.

> Affirm every answer, if possible, and draw out the participants by asking for clarification. Your aim is to make them feel comfortable sharing their ideas and learning, so be extremely hesitant to "shut down" a group member's contribution or "trump" it with your own. This does not mean, however, that you shouldn't correct false ideas—just do it in a spirit of gentleness and love.

> Don't allow a single person, or group of persons, to dominate the discussion. Involve everyone, if possible, and intentionally invite participation from those who are more reserved or hesitant.

> Labor to show the significance of their study. Emphasize the things that the participants could not have learned without doing the homework.

> Avoid talking too much. The group leader should not monopolize the discussion, but rather guide and shape it. If the group leader does the majority of the talking, the participants will be less likely to interact and engage, and therefore they will not learn as much. Avoid constantly adding the "definitive last word."

> The group leader should feel the freedom to linger on a topic or question if the group demonstrates interest. The group leader should also pursue digressions that are helpful and relevant. There is a balance to this, however: the group leader *should* attempt to cover the material. So avoid the extreme of constantly wandering off topic, but also avoid the extreme of limiting the conversation in a way that squelches curiosity or learning.

> The group leader's passion, or lack of it, is infectious. Therefore, if you demonstrate little enthusiasm for the material, it is almost inevitable that your participants will likewise be bored. But if you have a genuine excitement for what you are studying, and if you truly think Bible study is worthwhile, then your group will be

impacted positively. Therefore, it is our recommendation that before you come to the group, you spend enough time working through the homework and praying, so that you can overflow with genuine enthusiasm for the Bible and for God in your group. This point cannot be stressed enough. Delight yourself in God and in his Word!

✦ desiringGod

If you would like to explore further the vision of God and life presented in this book, we at Desiring God would love to serve you. We have thousands of resources to help you grow in your passion for Jesus Christ and help you spread that passion to others. At our website, www.desiringGod.org, you'll find almost everything John Piper has written and preached, including more than forty books. We've made over thirty years of his sermons available free online for you to read, listen to, download, and in some cases watch.

In addition, you can access hundreds of articles, find out where John Piper is speaking, learn about our conferences, and browse our online store. John Piper receives no royalties from the books he writes and no compensation from Desiring God. The funds are all reinvested into our gospel-spreading efforts. Desiring God also has a whatever-you-can-afford policy, designed for individuals with limited discretionary funds. If you'd like more information about this policy, please contact us at the address or phone number below. We exist to help you treasure Jesus Christ and his gospel above all things because he is most glorified in you when you are most satisfied in him. Let us know how we can serve you!

Desiring God
Post Office Box 2901 Minneapolis, Minnesota 55402
888.346.4700   mail@desiringGod.org